AGAMEMNON

THE FALL OF THE HOUSE OF USHER

STEVEN BERKOFF

AGAMEMNON

THE FALL OF THE HOUSE OF USHER

AMBER LANE PRESS

All rights whatsoever in these plays are strictly reserved and application for performance, etc. must be made before rehearsals begin to:

Rosica Colin Ltd
1 Clareville Grove Mews
London SW7 5AH

No performance may be given unless a licence has been obtained.

Originally published in 1977 by
John Calder (Publishers) Ltd.

This edition published in 1990 by
Amber Lane Press Ltd
Cheorl House
Church Street
Charlbury, Oxon OX7 3PR
Telephone: 0608 810024

Printed in Great Britain by
Richard Clay Ltd, Bungay, Suffolk

Copyright © Steven Berkoff, 1977, 1990

ISBN 1 872868 01 0

INTRODUCTION

Writer's Note

These plays were written to exorcise certain demons struggling within me to escape. *Agamemnon* is filtered through my own impressions of Greece and is rooted more in the elements of landscape, and sea . . . It is about heat and battle, fatigue, the marathon and the obscenity of modern and future wars. Naturally it is also about the body and its pleasures / pains. I have followed Aeschylus but chose to take my own route from time to time. Events smudge into each other and I have used from the Feast of Atreus the ghastly origins of the curse. This is a suitably horrific beginning, though horror was not what I wanted but a revelation of the crime. I described it as if it had happened to me, the final text was evolved after a long workshop series when the actors turned themselves into athletes, soldiers, horses and chorus. The text was chanted, spoken, sung and simply acted. I am really grateful particularly to two actors (Wolf Kahler and Barry Philips) who started on the first day (some time in April 1973) and finished with me on the 21 Aug 1976 and have been through each reworking and performance and gave the production the power and hard edge that it needed. Without them the play would never had reached the heights that I felt it did. David Toop and Paul Burwell created the music and welded themselves into the action like a cunning embroidery, constantly stimulating and inspiring. And thanks Deborah Norton for giving your electrifying voice and presence to Clytemnestra.

The Fall of the House of Usher is about energy twisted in upon itself. It is about the refined last stages of obsessive madness. It is delirium of the senses and is well enough described in the commentary that goes with the round by round description of the play.

Producer's Note

The following plays were performed by the *London Theatre Group;* a collection of actors welded together by a common purpose. To express drama in the most vital way imaginable; to perform at the height of one's power with all available means. That is, through the spoken word, gesture, mime and music. Sometimes the emphasis on one, sometimes on the other.

At first, in searching for material for these plays, I found the finished play to finite a form, simply a mass of dialogue, with no resonances of inner life, where the actors hurled situational chat at each other. Far more inspiration came from the short story form, or classic text, which gave the whole situation, the inner and outer life and subjective thought of the characters. Here the environment constantly shifts in the same way that the processes of the imagination can take you outside the boundaries of time and space. In fact, we worked closer to music and the scenario of the film. Instead of a dead setting on the stage fixing us firmly in the conscious world of the now the actor became the setting and the environment. His body, his voice and his text were made into a language malleable to swift changes of situation.

We always attempted an analysis of the play rather than a realistic rendering. Realism can eventually have a deadening effect since it only mirrors a conscious world and is more suited to TV drama. What we attempted in the following plays was a grotesque, surreal, paranoiac view of life such as is conjured up in dreams. . .the schizoid personality of man as he undoubtedly is. . .and the staging took on this manner in its exaggerated and enlarged forms. Naturalism, both in the writing and performing of plays, often leaves me with pangs of embarrassment, especially when witnessing actors playing this game of pretence. What we sought for was a critical analysis where we performed what was unreal and not perceivable in everyday life, and expressed drama less through impersonation than through revelation, hoping that a greater degree of reality would be shown by these methods.

STEVEN BERKOFF
1977

Photograph: Roger Morton

Agamemnon

*Freely adapted
from the Aeschylus version*

Agamemnon was first performed as work in progress at the Round House in December 1973.

The cast were:

AGAMEMNON	Steven Berkoff
CLYTEMNESTRA	Teresa D'Abreu
WATCHMAN/AEGISTHUS	Wolf Kahler
HERALD	Barry Philips
CASSANDRA	Anna Nygh
PARIS	Hilton Mcrae
HELEN	Shelley Lee
Legend of the Curse spoken by	Terrance McGinity
VILLAGE GOSSIP	Alfred Michelson
CHORUS	The whole cast plus: Joa L'Avila
MUSIC	Gordon Phillips
PRODUCTION	Steven Berkoff

This version of *Agamemnon* was first performed at the Greenwich Theatre in July 1976.

The cast were:

AGAMEMNON	Steven Berkoff
CLYTEMNESTRA	Deborah Norton
WATCHMAN/AEGISTHUS	Wolf Kahler
HERALD	Barry Philips
CASSANDRA	Anna Nygh
PARIS	Hilton Mcrae
HELEN	Shelley Lee
Legend of the Curse spoken by	Terrance McGinity
CHORUS	The whole cast plus: Day Murch, Lawrence Held and Matthew Scurfield
MUSIC	Paul Burwell David Toop
LIGHTING	John Gorringe
PRODUCTION	Steven Berkoff

LEGEND OF CURSE

Something begins to smell in this vile house/ is it
the stew/vomit-heaved that lies drying on the cracked
streets/ or in the dark cellar forgotten and growing
mushrooms from the slime/ under the lid/ life stirs from
the dead/ pot of stew crammed with bits of human flesh/
a finger or two slipped in by the neglectful cook who
was so careful to disguise the hell kitchen of skinned and
sliced torso with thick sauce/ sipping gently at first like
licking vomit/ strange already/ rot skunk stink/ like garlic
stuffed/ camouflage with bitter herbs the smell of pain/
who would know/ what laughs and female giggles hide
behind the dead teeth watching/waiting to belch out and
spit words with a Ha! Ha! You old rotting beast it's on
your own flesh that you feast/still/ quiet/ the faces
watching your face/ squaring its hole/ and down the gut
it rolls/ tendon calf lips even you, have kissed when
little/ the shoulder that you squeezed with comforting
grip/ the tongue that whistled/ bite/ gulp/ slither down/
that's gone for ever. The mouth opens again. That dark
chamber of horrors/ blind 'O' open and close/ open
and close stuffing down its own juices/ strange tasting
difficult to go down/ does gristle stick in throat/
some wine/ the gravy's very thick/ with blood/ your
own/ all move in slow motion/ the eyes stare/ fixed/
time stopped/ plates full not eating only you (around the
table) only you. It's very warm. The hand moving its
heavy beat/ from plate to faces/ as faces caught/ teeth
clenched jaws/ staring/ frozen fresco Why?/ It's hot/ the
garlic's strong/ loosen my clothes/ the smell/ why that
smell/ why still/ chews on/ on scrawny bone splintered
hard/ explore the mouth/ retrieve that bone belonging to
no animal I know/ the faces now slope in/ incline those
dark holes in their head to feast on you/ I know it now/
now it I know/ I am the feast they feast on/ my eternal
horror/ I know where are my little ones/ inside/ they're
sliding down my guts/ along the lengthy graves of my
intestines/ I know it now/ the thing retrieved from out
my nauseous mouth is topped with its little nail/ the
moon just rising. The heads of those that sloped/
hang/ taking no breath waiting for … the earth
appeared to stop … still … everything hung at the
end of that horror on my fork/ expecting me to break/
sob/ heave/ scream/ swallow my own beating heart/

tear hair/ stab my jellied eyes/ but no/ I'll show them
only how much I enjoy their rancid crime/ I'll show them
nothing/ take another glass of wine/ another forkful of
my baby/ as the vomit rises in my throat I'll force it
back/ and stuff it down with more/ the faces start to
shift/ incline a hairsbreadth back/ across their teeth the
smile begins to fade/ query in the dead eyes/ is he
already insane/ gone/ dead/ does he know?/ And still the
regular beat as hand digs plate and father takes back
dearest in broken pieces/ hand made meat/ but volts
inside the brain compute from horror/ multi-faceted
revenge (as mouth with pearl of vomit sneaking out the
corner/ finger dabs it back) A curse is being laid and
planned and grown in soil fertiled with heavy blood and
silently the curse matures in hate's loathsome brine and
shrieks its prayers to the gods/ in sounds too loud for
any mortal ears to hear/ but at the speed of light/
waves invisible already grip those horror thoughts/
ascend to heaven/ while the eyes revealing nothing nod/
the tongue continues to push its gushing vomit back/
the faces now are sunk into their heads/ not compre-
hending/ not knowing!! A napkin pats the lips/ a smile/
the chair scrapes back/ thank you for dinner/ they stare
into your fast receding back/ he wants to shout you to
the facts that you already carry in your bowels/ 'you've
eaten your own flesh you beast'. But tongue is locked
within the jaws/ and grits his teeth/ until like clay/
crumble/ break/ decay/ his lips stretch/ expose a smile/
more a stinking yellow smudge of pain/ the joke has not
quite teeth enough to bite/ between the cracks already a
seed of death begins to grow/ a little root will send its
veins and branches cracking through his skull/ through
all that flows from out his tainted blood/ from out his
loins/ his seed will poison/ all its flowers/ with a curse/
planted in that house/ that day/ hot afternoon/ when
the earth seemed to halt/ and eyes were locked/ on the
teeth of a fork.
The curse of the house of Atreus.

Song of Lineage and Events

This is Argos/ Argos is a clean city/ this is Agamemnon's
city/ Agamemnon son of Atreus/ ruler/ husband of
Clytemnestra/ he sailed the seas to Troy/ to kill that boy/
Paris/ who stole what wasn't his to take/ Helen/
Menelaus' mate/ Agamemnon murdered his own child/ a

sacrifice/ to calm the seas/ so wild/ for his Armada of
death/ Clytemnestra vows to avenge the bloody deed/
and on it goes/ without an end/ the curse first laid on
the house of Atreus.

Watchman

WATCHMAN. I watch night after night/ skin my eyes/
scan the skies/ look for a sign/ watchman watching/
stay alert/ the queen demands/ the first to see that
fire leaping/ will tell her/ Troy is taken/ that sign's
a code for victory/ a beacon's flare from isle to
isle/ some hope/ I long to go/ like me are other
watchers on those isles/ staring into space or are
they mad from boredom?

CHORUS. Don't dare to move/ you are part of an act
of fate/ stay alert/ stick to your post/ concentrate.

WATCHMAN. Ten years I've rotted on this watch/
cannot believe they've broken down those Trojan
walls/ and if they have/ smashed down the doors/
see her again/ some young whore who must be old
and poxy now/ they'll say it wasn't worth it after
all/ No! My mind is seeing visions/ no longer sure/
is that a light I see/ is it real or am I finally insane/
is it a dream/ or do I dance . . . for joy . . .
is it . . . no! . . . oh no! . . . It's out! Wait/ I do! . . .
It's there again/ yes/ I see it/ grow/ a little spit of
light/ but swelling and it's waving to me/ yes!
Shout out the news to Agamemnon's queen/ Troy
is fallen/ awake and sing!!

Song

CHORUS. Ten years since Agamemnon and Menelaus
hard men/ iron might of Atreus/ equipped in
deadly steel/ a thousand ships to the doom of Troy/
screaming like eagles/ maddened for the prey/
their nest pillaged/ clawed hate/ wings beating,
they swooped/ they ripped and tore/ the gods above
heard the furore/ their song of blood stung the air/
and so the house of Atreus swept on to crush the
house of Priam.

Battle One

Two Brave Soldiers

I am fighting for Troy
I am fighting for Greece
Your blood soaks me
Your sword is my pain
Your skin tears iike silk
I am fighting for Troy
I am fighting for Greece
You are killing me brother
You are killing me . . . .

CHORUS. For Paris and his body's lust/
A mile of sweet young flesh was hacked/
Javelins a splinter
Knees hit the dust/ Trojans drowning in each
other's blood/
Bones shattered at first clash/
Mouths turn to rust.

HELEN *and* PARIS *emerge from the chaos.*

PARIS. Helen! *(High sung soprano)*
Your hair is the colour of sun/
Your mouth has the taste of music/
Your thighs disturb my dreams/
I enter you/ as I enter temples carved
from marble tombs/ I float through your body/
Through velvet passages/ paintings of the future
line your walls/ your mouth devours me.

Image of HELEN *and* PARIS *together.*

CHORUS. He saw her being pinioned by his thrusting
strokes/ exchanging sweat and stink/ with tattoos
of their nightly games/ the Trojan boy who
kidnapped her will be paid with thrust for thrust/
Exchange cold steel for rape hard flesh/ steel
does not wilt/ insatiate weapon/ paying interest
in its piercing blessings/ hard lovers of Argos/
Ten thousand men/ ten thousand times/ will
Trojan bellies open up to them.

CHORUS. Javelin/ arrow/ spear/ sword/ axe/ cut/
thrust/ tear/ bleed/ hack!

Battle Two

CLYTEMNESTRA. *(Watching)*
  My husband is in Troy
  He has left me.
  He is a memory that is faulty/ he is desire that is
  curdled/ stride through my body Aegisthus/ send
  your armies through my veins.

AGAMEMNON. *(From the battle)*
  I am in Troy/ I have left her/ she is a memory that
  is faulty/ she is desire curdled/ I float in heat and
  blood/ I stride through men's flesh like cancer/
  my hands are the claws of eagles.

CHORUS. *(In present)*
  Meanwhile we wait/ for years we wait/ for
  Agamemnon for a sign/ senile carcasses spitting age
  and half-existence tottering on three legs/ while the
  men that stand on two are gone/ we chew our
  memories with boneless gums/ recall a day some
  years ago . . . .

CHORUS. *(In past)*
  Two leaders/ one in thought/ with a forest of
  spears/ in thousands pointing north/ scented the
  distant blood of Troy.

  The sound of the pulling of giant oars.

  Sea is the colour of paradise/
  Sea is the colour of Helen's eyes/
  The sea's depths are the deep unconscious
  That drag over our stone and wear us down to sand/
  The bodies of Helen drag the stiff agony out of our
  flesh/ she draws our blood/ the waves whisper
  her name/ drawing us to our death/ we live in her
  blood/ in her waves we twist and thresh/ woman
  wears us down to sand/ we die between her thighs/
  sea is the colour of paradise/ out of the sky an eagle
  dives/ and struck at a running hare ripping the wet
  blind young from its swollen belly/ so Agamemnon
  ripped open the belly of Troy/ sea is the colour of
  paradise.

CLYTEMNESTRA. Blood will feed on blood/
  The Gods will seek revenge/
  They will loathe the eagles glutting
  Winged beasts/ pinions sticky with blood/

Blood builds a tower of hate/
Mad blood raging to destroy/ its source/
In seeking vengeance of my child's life.

CHORUS.   There was a day in Aulis
When no ships would sail
And Agamemnon raged for a good Troyward wind/
Time bent double/ and the men grew stale . . . .

Sea wind and ship.

AGAMEMNON.   Where is the captain of the fleet/
Lash yourself to helm and mast/
The wind must change/ it must
My great fleet rotting in a foul wind/
Ropes rot/ Deserters slink away/ stare at the
white roofs day after day/ Armed men mope
along the shore and curse the wind and eat my
dwindling stores/ My warlike warriors are
withering fast/ Hoist yourself to helm and mast!

CHORUS.   The seas like waves of great iced claws/
the colour of phlegm/ stern hawsers hold us fast
or we'd be mashed by them.

CHORUS.   The seas like vast shaking mountains/
Roaring jelly/ A great thick milky/ squash/ wind
stung wave into a deadly froth.

CHORUS.   The seas like green paste/ whipped into a
curdled rage/ twisting our bowels/ our fleet spun
fore and aft/ top sail smacks barque.

AGAMEMNON.   What must I do/ what remedy?

CHORUS.   The prophet says/ to turn the wind there
must be a sacrifice/ a thought to crush like lead/
a maid must bleed/ on the altar stone/ do it/
the Gods demand/ your daughter must stain the
ocean red.

CLYTEMNESTRA.   My daughter's life to help a war for
a faithless wife!

AGAMEMNON.   Woman you/ what can I say/ Disaster
follows if I disobey.

CLYTEMNESTRA.   Worst disaster I promise you/
If you yield and slaughter/ my own child/ bloody
your hand in that virgin blood.

AGAMEMNON.   Either way ruin/ disband the fleet/

earn the deserter's badge/ betray the alliance now/
Apollo show me a way/ I drown in blood whichever
way I turn/ this web I cannot break.

CHORUS. He chose his course
They bared her throat to the cruel knife/
Wait!/ She cries in the wind her father's name/
Gag her mouth/ a sailor's dirty rag stuffed in her
throat/ no curse must fall/ rough hands tear off
her saffron silks/ her eyes did pierce us all/ her
murderers with, why?/ The vision passes/ I see
no more.

CLYTEMNESTRA. I see/ I always see/ her moans
echoed with the gulls who pitied her/ then those
brave men lifted the noble offering like a pig to
slaughter/ her golden body naked as the wind that
gently kissed her/ her round belly/ a soft cave
for babies/ not sharpened steel/ not to be ripped
open for vulture's beaks to fill/ the sea turned red as the
veins released their spurts and jets as the knife
twists in the hurt flesh/ already feasting are the
flies/ on drops of crimson red.

CHORUS. Show no more/ the future will show us
what's in store/ don't hunt for misery/ it will call
on you without invitation/ speak only of good/
shut the horrors behind the door/ if they seep
through the cracks/ then seal the cracks/ if they
crawl through the pores/ no say no more/ here
comes our Lady Clytemnestra.

CHORUS. Great and lovely queen/ royal majestic/
have you some news?/ Please tell us what you
know/ News/ what/ news / how/ she knows
something/ What?/ Shh!/ Let us hear/ What/
Hmmm?/ What????/ What????

CLYTEMNESTRA. Our armies have taken Troy.

CHORUS. What? How? Did she say? Believe that?
No way!

CLYTEMNESTRA. The Greeks have taken Troy/ Is
that clear?

CHORUS. Ooh yes? When/ how/ When please/ When?

CLYTEMNESTRA. This very night before this glorious
day.

CHORUS. Ha! Ha! Ha! Ha! Who told you that, last
         night! No one travels so fast/ No God travels so
         fast/ News travels fast/ but not that fast/ What
         travels so fast?/ Ha ha ha ha!

CLYTEMNESTRA. Fire travels/ Fire speaks/ The God
         of fire raced from peak to peak/ The God of fire
         leapt/ scorched crackles and shrieks/ I had a
         hundred watchmen trained for years on highest
         peaks/ from here to Troy/ to light their fires when
         they see the smoke begin to rise from Trojan
         streets/ their eyes they focussed on infinity did
         not dare blink! They must not miss the faintest
         whisp that tells them something's burning/
         something lives on fire/ the tunnel in the water
         of their eyes must pass the picture back to me/
         Fire's my sign/ the sign they pass to me/ from Ida
         Lemnos/ Athos/ Skyros/ across the Agean Sea/
         A whip lash of lightning like molten gold/ the
         sharks danced to see the beacons glow/ each/
         sleepy watchman fired his sticks in turn/ so a
         current of flame streaked over Euripus/ hill to hill/
         crackle scorch and burn/ it soared it swung it came/
         like an avenging angel across a frozen forest of
         stars/ Aesopus/ it burned on to Kitheron/ burn/
         the great marsh of Gorgopis/ burn burn burn/
         raced on like fiery stallions to Aegyplantus peak/
         lightning strokes lit the skies/ jagged veins of
         flame/ dancing fireflies/ then shook its beard of
         shimmering red/ leapt headlong across the Saronic
         Gulf until at last/ on Arachnus burst into bloom/
         then flew like a meteor/ on to the house of Atreus/
         my fire runners ran/ relay to relay/ unbroken/ my
         marathon of flame/ that is my news/ what have you
         to say?

CHORUS. Thanks to the Gods for this great day/ Tell
         us more/ if more you have to say?

CLYTEMNESTRA. Today the Greeks hold Troy/ a strong
         embrace you may believe/ her neck is broken by his
         amorous grip/ defeat and triumph rend the air in
         sounds that will not blend/ untuneful discord grates/
         I think I hear the wailing of women hugging dead
         ones/ dear ones hacked/ familiar faces resculptured
         by the indelicate surgery of the bloody knife/
         Lovers frozen in their agony grin/ with dead

teeth/ hands outstretched for the last embrace/
like dead branches/ trembling/ fingers search the
death masks for familiar faces/ children shake the
stiffening corpses/ I think the smell of death that
rises from the streets/ rising from the swelling
carcasses will be horrible/ the smell of death is
always horrible/ mothers say 'Sons?'. . .
Babies cry 'Mama?' All dead/ gone/ nameless/
sharing that smell/that horrible reek/ while the
crows patiently wait/ is my husband still alive/
Does he walk through the smell that's rising/
will he bring it home with him/ The Greeks that
live drunk with gore/ grind the last painful drops
of strength from those proud women/ isn't it
what victors do/ snatch their fill in soft beds/
while their owners sleep quietly in their own pools
of blood/ is it not what victors do/ snatch tear and
roam/ hungry hands/ ten years hungry seek out
satisfaction/ hot soft satisfaction/ satiate yourselves /
be satisfied but leave the shrines standing you
victors/ the Gods may be watching you/ the long
journey back is still to come/ dying curses carry
far/ who listens out there in space/ who watches
you/ for blood in the earth cries for blood/
my dearest wish is that peace exists.

Revolt

CHORUS.   The people mutter against these leaders/ for
each widowed bed/ fatherless child/ an angry hate
prevails/ to send our youth to battle/ for political
strife/ from grief springs gall/from this grows
venom/ why should we be turned to ash for another's
lousy wife.

CHORUS.   Blood will have blood *(Repeat into march
rhythm)* The high will fall/ the ghosts of men who
died for nothing/ will walk and wail by a ruined
wall.

CHORUS.   Since the beacon's news was heard/
Rumours fly through every street/
Believe that?/ Believe a word of that mad woman/
cracked brain deceit/ fire can lie/ facts change/
Fantasies of a beacon's blaze/ Words of a woman
are quickly spread/ and as you know are quickly
dead/ I think I see a dot begin to grow into
something moving/ slow/ now fast/ now faster still/

it's shape suggests a man running/ telling us/ what?/
Chaos/ disaster/ more?/ A herald running from the
shore.

CHORUS.   *(Song matches rhythm of runner seen at a
great distance)*
Where there over there/ Where there over there/
Where there/ Where there/ Where there/ See him now/
Where/ See him now/ Where/ Nearly there/ Nearly there/
Ten nine eight seven six five four three two/ Oh
you're nearly there/ Oh! you're nearly there/ two
two/ two/ one you're there/ you're there/ you're
there . . . .

HERALD *runs on the spot accompanied by
vocalisation of* CHORUS. *He then runs silently.
We get the impression that he has run for miles to
deliver this news. His heart is bursting. He stops.*

HERALD.   On this good soil of Argos/ I never dared to
dream that I would see my blessed earth again/
Great Agamemnon's coming back/ render him the
welcome he deserves/ Troy has toppled down/ her
shrines dissolved in dust/ her seed exterminated by/
chattering machines of death that spit from iron
mouths/ by the hot breath of napalm/ scorching
the sins that stank to heaven/ while howitzers
screeched arias in the streets/ Ack Ack/ Ack Ack/
and dumb-dumb shells explode/ their scattering
claws of steel explore mens' veins and arteries/
and spread confusion in flying brains/ and guts
that fell like hail and slimed the roofs/ a panoply
of armour ripped the sky apart/ as Zeus unleashed
missile after missile/ and anti missile missile missile/
equal to the weight of ten thousand tons of hate/
ploughed the fields/ destroyed the crops/ forever/
lay waste even the waste/ bore holes the size of
mountains/ while our brave boys/ burning under a
monstrous sun/ and seizing what they had/ gleaming
bazookas/ Patton\tanks like Trojan horses made
from heavy steel/ rasped deadly snorts into the
walls/ which fell like flaking skin/ that's nuclear
scorched/ and Zeus laughed and laughed and spat
out deadly gasses from his guts/ and men collapsed
like flies/ heaved out their entire wet insides/ we
sloshed around a slaughter house of guts/ then
in we marched/ with masks of death/ protected
'gainst that burning breath around us/ grasping in

fists our automatics proudly cocked/small fat
grenades packed in our crutch/ and ricocheted
around the town our tuneful whistling bullets/
smooth bore/ cannon/ trench/ mortar/ shrapnel/
tommy gun/ and blow pipe/ **RAT TAT TAT TAT/
RAT TAT TAT TAT/ KA BOOM/ KA BLAST/
KA BLAM/ SPLAT! PHUTT! SMASH! PHAM!!!
WOW!** Watch! them! Watch them! Stampede
of footless bodies/ trailing like snails/ their
last remaining drops of bloody spore/ for
target practice we took them/ and watched them
as they clawed the walls/ and cried Ma Ma with
lipless mouths/ then slid into their raw and running
juices/ Meanwhile outside the town/ beneath the
deep/ and surfacing like black and angry sharks/ a
fleet of submarines/ torpedo boats with armour/ so
intense/ it hurts to speak it/ gun boats too/ in
skins of iron opened their deadly jaws/ and belched
a hail of delayed action fission shells/ to mop up
what we leave/ and soften little knots of fierce
resistance/ huddled in the hills like scorpions/ and
watched them fry alive in holes/ and then our king/
our Agamemnon/ in the front/ with only his bare
hands/ and at his side ringing against their skulls
like truth/ his sword and sabre/ rapier/ scimitar
and cutlass/ dagger/ battle-axe and mace/ his trusted
knuckle-duster that he likes/ just all good plain
steel/ cold hard honest naked steel/ he kept on
never tiring/ all alone except a regiment or two to
keep him company/ deter annoying hands from
bothering him/ with toys that spray at lightning
speed fine strands of steel/ that slice to ribbons all
unfortunates that go too near our king/ our beloved
and holy Agamemnon/
It's over now/ the dead will never rise again/ no
point in crying over life's unkindness/ pack up
your troubles/ our losses do not balance out our
gains/ give thanks to God for what he's won/ my
speech is done.

CLYTEMNESTRA. My fire sign gave me the truth/
came streaking through the night/ to tell me/
what you now cram in your ears/ like hungry
mouths/ you took me for a wandering fool/ as I
made sacrifice in every corner of the town/ with
bags of herbs and incense/ burning for his return/
him/ my famous husband's coming back/ what
sweeter vision for a woman/ unlock the gates/ her

man's returned/ safe from the wars/ I'll see his
face/ hold it in my hands/ and whisper in his ear/
my darling of the town/ your woman's waited for
you/ faithful as you left her/ your own sweet
palace watchdog/ fierce to other hands/ loyal only
to yours/ I'll have my maids prepare a bath/ for
your tired bones/ from jasmine/ juniper and
hyacinth leaves/ and sponge your wounds/ and
wash away the dirt and pain of Troy/ from each
and every pore/ and clean away that death smell/
that might linger in your hair until you rise as
white as marble cherubim/ as soft as persimmon
skins/ and smelling like a garden after rain has
poured her nectar through its wild profusions/
and your golden skin shall lie between me and soft
sheets/ my hands will find your body where it's
sweet/ and melt the years away/ in kisses/ hot/
wild and deep/ I've kept your seal intact all these
long years/ revealed to no man else what's solely
thine/ could no more breathe a breath of shame
my man than I could dip hot steel.
Go and tell him/ this . . . .
Before you go/ just one word more/ Menelaus/
you quite forgot to say/ what happened to the
other half of Agamemnon.

HERALD. Not quite so fortunate/ a storm did hit the
fleet/ the first day out/ the last crap on the beach/
the sails repaired/ hoist up the rig/ release the
hawsers/ a soft wind fills our sails/ like the giant
cheeks of Cyclop's ass/ all's well/ the sea's as calm
as thick as syrup/today the sky a halcyon sheet of
baby blue/ deceptive calm/ too quiet/ this smooth
untroubled stillness/ eyes claw the skies/ same
small puff of wind/ so gently pushing us out/ as if
perhaps into the ring . . . then one black night/ we
felt a team of elephants begin to move beneath our
bows/ that sudden lurch which brings our supper
foully back into our mouths/ *(Sound of ship's bell)*
The sea began to boil and rage/ and waves the size
of cliffs came roaring at us/ ship's smashed ship
like butting rams/ stampeding/ still it raged and
foamed/ old Neptune's nightmares make him
thrash around down deep/ in some infernal
tortured sleep/ whilst up/ the sky fell down in
chunks of hail like bullet spray/ and screamed and

howled/ white veins of lightning twisted on its face/
and in each neon flash/ we saw our faces whiter than
the scathing foam/ then suddenly it stopped/ old
fishy Neptune turned around/ went back to sleep/
the stars peeked out again behind the scuddering
clouds/ and blinked a bit/ as if not sure/ and as the
dawn rose we saw the Aegean thick with bloated
Greeks/ like flowers scattered by the wind/ and
lazy sharks unbelieving their good luck/ were having
breakfast/ the fleet was smashed except for us/ we
sailed through that infernal nightmare/with
not one timber sprung.

The Celebration

CHORUS *enact ceremony, welcome back gestures,*
shaking of hands, congratulations etc. They pat the
HERALD *who bounces like a ball: home boy returns.*

CHORUS. *(Could be spoken by single member of*
        CHORUS*)*
        Have you not seen the end of evil/ the end of pride/
        will you stick your fingers to your head/ when some
        ass-hole with a stripe slithers by/ will you stick
        your fingers in the fire/ it's just the same/ just as
        stupid and futile/ no more horrors/ widows/
        orphans/ crippled/ blinded/ butchered/ burnt and
        slain/ no more victims/ mournings/ terror/ tortures/
        execution/ pain/ no more soldiers/ warriors/
        uniforms/ weapons/ ass-licking for gain/ no more
        queens/ kings/ generals/ princes/ ministers/
        dictators/ no more slaying for them/ no more
        horrors/ bandages/ hospitals/ waiting/ crying/
        letters/ sorry to inform you/ no more/ no more of
        them/ no more coffins/ grave yards/ flowers/
        black robes/ caused by them . . . no more horrors . . . .

(He repeats the speech from "No more horrors . . ."
until the blackout and the drum beat, that announces
the arrival of AGAMEMNON, *cuts him off.)*

Agamemnon

*We hear him arrive. A troop of horses (the chorus in
elongated horse masks and shod feet) begins very slowly
(like the herald) and grows faster and faster. The horses
group tightly and expand (much as a film of horses seen
in the distance,) they canter and they gallop. As they tire
some horses drop out or collapse from exhaustion. It continues and the sound grows louder. It is the sound of the word
AGAMEMNON, repeated and broken and hurled into the
air like thunder. Ten years and at last he is here. The
entrance should suggest this. Music and drums, brass
instruments screaming. It still goes on. CHORUS members
may die in this enactment and must not take part unless
they have strong hearts. In order to reach the town they
whip and beat each other. At last they slow down,
allowing, naturally, AGAMEMNON to take the lead.
They slow down to a slow-motion and deliberately
stately entrance. We see that AGAMEMNON has a
captive tied to a rope which is round her neck. This is
CASSANDRA. To make more of his return it would be
wise to let AGAMEMNON in prior scenes be played by
a surrogate or memory.*

CHORUS. Welcome great Agamemnon/ stormer of
     Troy/ what can we say/ except our joy in seeing
     you is great/ I will not smile/ with masks concealing
     twisted thoughts/ nor grovel in the dirt to sing
     your praise/ but speak our honest thoughts/ we
     had/ I do confess a shred or two of doubt/ when
     you (as well as other gallant friends) adventured
     to destroy a *Nation!*/ and some few thousand of
     our gallant boys to bite the dust/ and be manure
     for the weeds/ all for the sake of one young girl/
     but/ all is well now and the work well done! You
     know us/ we're for you Agamemnon.

AGAMEMNON. First I hail Argos and her Gods who
     know the right course from the wrong/ receive from
     me the conqueror's greeting on my safe return/ your
     wrath sent justice through my arms to break great
     Troy/ and doom her walls to dust/ and send to
     Hades those worshippers of pride, theft and lust/
     we did not fight alone/ nor smash those walls with
     just our armoured fists/ since God was by our side/
     and in the field/ he raged with us/ and whispered

in my ear/ be ruthless Argive lions/ and make
them pay for their proud rape/ give them hell you
bastards/ don't let one bitch escape/ and so at
dead of night we spilled from out the guts of our
great horse/ to grind the city's bones/ then sprang/
a swarming pride of hungry lions/ tore/ swept/
pounced/ licked Trojan blood and killed/ her
smoking spirals still ascend to heaven/ to mark this
planet's bloody sore/ which painfully we cauterised/
we lanced the pus from out the boil/ her perfumed
lust and painted glory/ rise in a storm of ashes/ but
it was justly sent/ the immortals cast the votes
into an urn marked/ death/ that is the law/ I do
not ask for more/ now the Gods are thanked I turn
to you/ I know you/ I know how false your loves
can be/ when envy of another's fortune grips your
heart/ I know you/ your runny eyes/ that never
look at man straight/ but bend a little on the way/
in case they may expose a palsied thought or two/
only one man was not a backstabber/ had faith in
me alone/ no unctuous bullshit sprouting from his
gob/ and that was Ulysses!!! Inventor of that
wooden charging steed/ armed to the teeth/ with
belly full of iron and steel/ and *men!*/ with desperate
bloody hunger to fulfill/ I see from your glaucous
blinking stares that cancers have been grown here/
that may require the knife and white hot iron/ to
purge the body for its good/ I go now to my home
and hearth/ a drop of wine/ a friendly bath/ is what
I need/ all simple things/ you see/ I'm just a simple
man.

CLYTEMNESTRA. *(She has arrived to meet him, but
they are distant from each other in space.)*
I rose today at dawn and watched the sea/ I knew
you would be there/ the wind was fresh/ the
curtains blew onto my face/ and through the gauze
I thought I saw your sail/ or was it just a fishing
boat that dipped and weaved/ but something
inexplicable told me it was a rhythm I recognised as
yours/ and now I can see you standing there/ so
strong/ so many years have I waited for my man/
desolate/ a prey to every rumour in the wind that
telegraphs your picture in my mind with stab
wounds/ broken bleeding by some Trojan wall/
and then I'd leap into a noose and be cut down by

frightened slaves/ and then I'd try to drown
myself in tears/ I have been so alone and watched/
as when the master's gone/ the rats come out to
play/ prowling cut-throats/ desperate men,
agitators, subverters of the state/ creep out like
bone crunching hyenas in the night/ with only me
between them/ Ahh! Now it's over/ over it's now
Ahh!/ There is no lovelier sight in all the world but
you my own ship's anchor/ my towering king/
post that holds this house in place/ now let a path
of crimson silk be spread/ to lead you to the house
you feared you'd never see again/ step on/ crush
down my dear/ your carpet red!

AGAMEMNON.   My own dear wife/ I do believe you
missed me/ you said so in a speech almost as long
as my absence/ spare me your queenly dialogue/
your rather loud Italianate display/ apart from
stirring envy in the hearts of men/ as well as other
eyes that watch from satellites of God/ I am a man
and not a superstar playing twice nightly the
Acropolis/roll up here's ba boom and la di da!
I'm just a simple man.

CLYTEMNESTRA.   But then you would upset me/
Upset my well meant plan.

AGAMEMNON.   I only mean to say you'll upset mine.

CLYTEMNESTRA.   Imagine Priam Conqueror, what
would he have done?

AGAMEMNON.   I can't/ he didn't win.

CLYTEMNESTRA.   Of eyes that watch don't be afraid/
you're a conqueror/ not a humble slave/ walk on
for me.

AGAMEMNON.   Why invite envy gossip hate/ invite
destruction by the aping of a God/ the sin of pride
is high.

CLYTEMNESTRA.   Just to please me/ if ever you loved
me/ but don't if you don't wish/ Agamemnon's mind
is his own/ isn't it dearest/ but if you did/ just this
time/ once/ this special time/ the dog star is high/
you must be very hot/ go inside now/ do not fear/
please/ we wait . . . / a little tiny movement it will
take.

AGAMEMNON. Who do we know is watching me as I
crush these silks into the courtyard's dirt.

CLYTEMNESTRA. Who can exhaust the sea that teems
with purple dye/ your return is like spring after
winter/ sun after rain/ pleasure after pain . . . .

(As AGAMEMNON *mounts the carpet)*

AGAMEMNON. Take in this girl and treat her kind/ she
came with us/ choice flower/ conquerors show
clemency in power.

(He mounts the ramp. CLYTEMNESTRA *lets out
a cry of triumph and goes inside with him.)*

CHORUS. Something beats against my heart like dread
tapping a remorseless code/ it's message black/
unbidden thoughts creep in/ unwanted yet they
gnaw away like rats tearing at our peace of mind/
he walks in his hour of triumph/ sinews taut/
voice clear/ champion of fate/ fist/ clenched and
gut hard/ against the odds he wins/ teeth bared in
victorious grimace/ he avoids the reefs/ he avoids
the arrows/ legs bestride his vanquished/ like a
Hercules.
So humanity strides on unaware of the germ that
grows within feeding on his vanity/ sucking at his
stem of life/ until one day/ he wakes to see his
body plagued by boils/pus streaked/fly blown/ and
wishes he had never been alive at all.

*(*CLYTEMNESTRA *and* AGAMEMNON. *Only the
two. Two chairs. They both face outwards.)*

CLYTEMNESTRA. What are you thinking/ of her? Was
her body nice to touch/ did it welcome you/
softly/ comforting/ did you break your rock hard
pain upon those soft/ thighs/ they opened lovingly/
her captive eyes would not close/ she wanted every
thing/ you sunk into her like a stone/ at night tired
after a day's killing/ she couldn't wait could she/
dried blood still on you/ not even wait to wash it
off/ was it so strong/ perhaps her tastes liked the
blood when you kissed her/ you drew blood/ the
violence of your slashing days infected the nights/
clashing teeth and tongues squirming/ I know/
that's how it once was with us/ was it not like that

once/ say yes/ go on say it was like that once/
don't deny me that as well/ so young she is/ very
tender as she held your precious appetite/ and your
locked limbs exchanged so many secrets/ and mute
demands/ did her body tell you what to do/ how/
speed/ where Oh where it's best my darling/ and
yes yes yes yes! And Oh the dried blood of some
poor slain boy that you cut down/ whose heart
and life you stopped for ever/ that blood running
off your cheeks in rivers of sweat/ your passion
and her blood/ and did she moan loud with her
open eyes that wanted everything/ did perhaps the
blood and sweat trickle onto her neck/ and a little
she tasted/ as it dropped gently down on her face
and her busy tongue excused itself to yours as
she gathered it up with the tip/ whilst far below
you were working/ busy stoker/ perhaps even making
plans for the future/ in her womb/ were the nights long/
enough for you.

AGAMEMNON.   I am so tired now/ suddenly I feel as
if I can no longer hear the words you say/the
years I spent away/crowd my head/with noise/
and music of the cries and clash of weapons/till I
no longer hear even my own thoughts/ what did
you say to me/ what do you want/ I thought I
heard you ask me to say something to you/ some
soft words/ about our ancient bed times/ I would
like to/ say something but when I try to think/ a
memory comes swimming in my head and tears
away the fragile pictures I retain of you/ what
did you say/ do you expect something/ your eyes
look as if they expect something/ they look empty/
dried up/ like you expect something from me/ that
will bring them to life again/ dried up pools/
scoured dry with bitterness/ I know/ you want a
word or two from me that will bring/ flooding
back into those withered circles/ tears/ life/
memories/ but as I try to frame a word or two
for you/ I try/ the other sounds come rushing
back again like sirens/ in my mind/ as if to flood
forever/ the distant empty years we had/ the
sounds we made are small/ I am so tired now/
prepare a bath for me/ and then perhaps I'll find
a word or two.

CLYTEMNESTRA *leaves him and returns
to* CASSANDRA.

CLYTEMNESTRA.   You! Come inside the house my
dear/ see how kind we are/ although a slave you
need not fear/ our slaves are kindly treated/ even
you/ can't you understand my words/ come come
don't stand there like a drunken whore/ and
wallow in your grief/ on you I'll waste no breath.

Exits

CHORUS. *(Watching* CASSANDRA*)* Does it speak/
can it understand/ an animal trapped/ as if sensing
danger sniffs the air/ who and why?/ Questions
fly around the corners of her eyes.

CASSANDRA. (*Slowly and carefully: the words
draining out of her with effort.*)
Apollo my God where have you led me/ what
house is this?

CHORUS.   Atreus/ the house of Atreus.

CASSANDRA.   God-hated house/ Oh no/ the smell
lingers/ the smell of butcheries/ dangling horror/
cries! What are those cries! This is a cursed house!

CHORUS.   No curse here/ who said anything about a
curse/ clean city/ no blood here/ clean walls/
Agamemnon's city.

CASSANDRA.   Cries in the night/ I hear them/ screams/
children/ carved/ babies/ the cries linger/ flesh
roasting/ fathers cramming their own flesh in their
hands/ all here here here/ Uuugh! Now the rancid
fumes rise/ I see her now/ slime encrusted
woman/ no no/ his ritual bath is full/ drag him
away! Drag him away!/ Washing him now/ washes/
while one hand searches behind her/ searches/ for
something!/ What?/ He white naked rising/ hot/
steam rising/ pounding her heart/ he must hear it! /
The female beast's heart smashes against her ribs
telling him/ he doesn't hear/ tell him/ tell him/
he smiles/ he looks/ doesn't see the net that's
closing in on him/ it falls/ falls/ trapped/ what! . . ./
his eyes rise to see her/ his eyes swivel on to
her/ too late/ trapped/ her hand gropes for the
knife/ fingers clawing for the hilt/ slipping both
on the wet floor/ Two hearts/ cow gores bull/ he
rises trapped in the web/ pulls tighter/ as he
struggles/ a tangle of flesh/ a hard stroke/ sunlit
blade/ it rises to strike and he sees there the sun's last

light/ lunge into the soft/ home/ crumbles/ his sad
whine/ like a slaughtered bull/ blood spray and both
sliding in his gore/ mouth gape and froth/ and
again/ she scatters his future years in bloody gore/
stinking slaughter house/ Oh weep/ cry and scream
a scorpion's rattle/ hear it/ laugh/ fester/ that cry
of triumph you slug of nature/ I see it all/ I see it/
I know I swear/ I prophesy ahead of time.

CHORUS.   She is insane or God-possessed.

CASSANDRA.   Not insane no/ they all say that to me/
I read your future lives/ Apollo's gift to me . . .
to scent out blood before and aft . . . .

CHORUS.   A gift to you/ what did you give to him?

CASSANDRA.   I lay down by the banks of Scamander
and he took me for his bride/ and poured his life
in me/ the Sun made love to me/ my soul he
set on fire/ and poured his light into my veins/
and each time he began again/it's like it never
ended/ a God feels no fatigue/ and sun shafts
penetrated me/ and I was floating down an
endless stream for ever and for ever/ then it grew
cold/ I woke to find the sun had slipped away/ he
had to go you see but left me with his sight/ to
always be a step ahead of human time/ I foresaw
the fall of Troy/ I read your future lives . . . time
and space are to me one . . . / I see your hour-glass
of death/ invade your eyes/ know how many seconds
you have left/ each and every one I breathe your
future breath/ smell your fears/ fright scums your
very breath/ lines your clothes/ you live like death
heads/ waiting for the moment/ . . . Agamemnon
my Lord dead/ dead/ dead/ in me lives his plant/
it pulls my womb/ it feels its father's waves . . .
stop/ cut off/ it moaned inside my belly/ I feel it
move/ knowing it's creator's stopped/ Agamemnon
dead/ then in I must go . . . dare I die with him/
make the stroke quick/ butcher woman/ make me
strong to face her . . . .

CHORUS.   If you see so much/ then you are brave/
brave woman/ going alone/ steps with courage to
the altar stone.

CASSANDRA.   I am going/ let the sun pour down one
last moment more upon my head/ how beautiful.

It is the strength of life/ poor humanity that can
be so easily stopped by the edge of a knife . . . .
(She exits)

A scream is heard.

CHORUS. The deed is done/ I fear/ quick in!!

CHORUS. Too late/ it is too late.

CHORUS. Catch her with the murder weapon steaming
in her hand.

CHORUS. No!

CHORUS. Why?

CHORUS. A plan is needed or we fail.

CHORUS. Talk and talk/ action is needed now.

CHORUS. No.

CHORUS. Why?

CHORUS. We must be certain whose scream.
It was the king/ kill her in the act.

CHORUS. Yes! *(All rush two steps.)*

CHORUS. But?

CHORUS. What??

CHORUS. We cannot bring him back to life.

CHORUS. True, so what do we do?

CHORUS. Think. Make our enquiries first.

CLYTEMNESTRA *enters.*

CLYTEMNESTRA. The thing is done/ Oh yes . . . long
overdue. A great while have I planned the trial of
strength to snare the beast and see my work
achieved/ I caught him in the net and watched him
squirm/ and try to tear his way from certain death/
a bundle of devouring hate did writhe when first
he sensed my sharpened blade cut at his life/ and
twisted like a trapped bear in the hunt/ could only
growl and whimper and as I drew back my blade
he whined for mercy/ then I pierced him twice/
the sack did buckle shriek and spew its blood from
out his mouth since I struck him true and deep/ and
then for luck I shoved the third and final thrust
deep in his guts/ then he retched forth his life/in

in one swift jet/ it's fountain soaked me in its
drizzle like spring rain from heaven/ I do not blush
to tell/ he then went down stiff and down he
F E L L!

CHORUS. The blood you shed will be yours one day/
another will come/ another will repay.

CLYTEMNESTRA. A waste of breath to mourn his
life/ the hand of justice held the knife.

CHORUS. Out of this house/ go/ out of this house/
Murderess/ out out out out out out out out!

CLYTEMNESTRA. You threaten me with exile/ you
were silent as the grave/ when for a wind this dead
dog tore my daughter's throat away/ you vile
mis-shapen swine could only stare and feebly
pray.

CHORUS. A filthy vulture hovers cawing/ on a corpse
its song of gloating.

CLYTEMNESTRA. I swear to you by my child's blood
and by the demon of hell to whom I now consign
Agamemnon's ghost/ that I am fearless when
Aegisthus stands strong as a rock on whom I
can rest my head/ this other piece of flesh/ lay
as was his habit/ bedded with his Trojan whore/
rather dead to enjoy the opportunity any more/
the sight will sharpen my future bed's delight.

CHORUS. Tarantula bitch has poisoned your life/ but
the curse of Atreus willed the knife.

AEGISTHUS *enters with a bull whip.*

AEGISTHUS. Silence dogs and listen hard/ learn/
unblock your wax/ feed information through your
rusty skulls and know this/ this man's father drove
my father from the land/ dispute about power/ we
ate misery/ we/ dust/ we crawled in the dirt/ years
later in hunger/ knees scraping the deck/ a beggar/
help me please brother/ we'll eat humble pie/ we'll
be no brother/ be my guest Atreus slimed/ eat and
enjoy/ reconciliation/ roast meat and wine/ but
the meat that was stewed was handmade human
child/ my small brothers/ he ate his own issue/ his
own darling flesh/ then Atreus showed him the
heads of the game he had devoured/ father said
nothing/ but his mind made secret contracts with

the Gods/ to plague this house in pain so thick
you'll burst/ I planned the play/ blood for blood/
slates clean/ OK!

CHORUS.   The tale of blood is not over/ it has only
just begun.

AEGISTHUS.   Eat the air/ hollow heads/ dreamers/
you'll do nothing but obey/your faces grey with
daily kvetch/ wasted/ muscle limp/ useless/ too
weak to fight/ toothless hags/ voices like women
croaking/ vanish bastards before my whip tears
shreds out of your asses!

CHORUS.   A sanctuary you have turned into a grave/
now I hear you crow and strut/ gorge on glutton/
sewer rat/ sneaking out in the night/ behind a
woman's petticoats you bite . . . .

CLYTEMNESTRA.   *(Restraining him from carrying out
his threat.)*   Ignore the mob/ they quake and quell/
you and I are in power darling/
we shall order things well . . . .

END

The Fall of the House of Usher

Play Adaptation
And Commentary on Production

With gratitude to Terry James for his initial inspiration
and help

Introduction to Poe and Performance

When this play works one lives on the crest of a wave when all elements fuse into a dynamic whole. Music, light, shape and words, then one is transported to another world as an actor and I hope as an audience . . . One is separated in this world as an alien theatrical species from whence you view the humanity that courses by . . . A strange metaphysical planet within whose body it is possible to be purged and scoured. To dwell within the world of Poe is to commit oneself to the self-imposed exile of the anchorite. To enter this confinement of senses painfully attenuated to vibrate to the slightest tremor of the outside or inside world is to discover the spirituality of Poe via his chorus, Roderick Usher. But since one is affected by this journey one may at the same time chart the spirituality within oneself. This exile demands constant fidelity; the playing out of Roderick Usher's arabesque fantasies each night permits no cheating and coruscates the days in a gentle wash of acid. All is dominated by the evening. All excesses are curbed . . . The temperament hones to the delicate knife edged sensitivity of Usher . . . whose senses 'are painfully acute'.

To play him is to know him. One cannot approach such a life as Usher's without absorbing his texture, by the quivering nature of a person who is all nerve endings . . . not so abnormal but wholly aware to the degree where life is no longer tolerable, where it can only be made tolerable by the deliberate blunting of the senses. This he is unprepared to do, necessary as it may be for the quotidian demands of everyday existence.

The tale of the impossible . . . A house with its own soul. A death. A resurrection. A moor's pestilential environment. A house that outwardly manifests the crumbling nature of Roderick's inner decay. A febrile fantastical story that served as an occult tale for our voices and senses, to find their expression through. The actors must be the house and its decaying fabric, must speak as stones and the memories of the house that are seared into its walls . . . must be the death rattle and atmosphere, must be the environment and since humans are born of the environment they must reflect it.

Breath is the wind and the cry the wind makes as it twists itself through the trees in a storm. The atmosphere is our lungs and the forests and branches our vocal cords. It is also the sound of ancient things groaning under the weight of age. It is not just a vehicle for words spoken at each other.

When Stanislavsky asked one of his actors to be a tree we now smile benevolently at these ruses to awake our imagery, these early formal experiments in acting. Yet now, more than ever, must we find our bodies in sympathy with nature . . . absorb it and express it . . . must be trees, sedges, windows, walls. Feel and express what is occupying the same earth as man and is germane to it.

In Usher, and for Poe, the elements pour into each other in a screaming confusion of nature at war with a decaying growth upon it that must die and be swallowed up . . . Poe's story with its main theme of incestuous love seems as much concerned with nature, and the sentience of things around him as it is with words, books and the phsychological confrontation, between order (the friend) and chaos (Usher).

Usher's chaos is the chaos in an organism about to die and a rush of life demonstrates its final outburst, like the amazing and frightening colours of a descending sun.

On Performing

Our bodies link, break away, dance, flow to each other passing these valuable segments of information . . . must be stretched, plastic, communicative. Mime demands exactness as any ritual must since it is mutually shared with the audience whose imaginative participation is required to make it live. Words are ours alone which they can take or leave or even read or translate or miss a word here and there. Not so with mime . . . If they lose concentration and hence the structure they lose themselves and their involvement . . . They cannot be surprised unless they are with us totally. If they wander from what we are doing they are lost.

On Audiences

The audience's ultimate climax is in catharsis. But catharsis is achieved only by the careful building up of events and the elimination of small and irrelevant detail . . . Imagination is the great rambling whale of the audience's mind that must be harpooned by the controlled imagination from the stage . . . it must be hooked, trapped and made one by the hypnotic power of the performers and their gestures . . . The spirit of magic and fairy tale should pervade the stage . . . legends and myths tap the dream world of the spectator. In his imagination or unconscious world lie much unexplained debris, fears and repression, anxieties and coded dreams. The need to explain this huge storehouse is made apparent in the myths that man has invented to chart the inner life. The need to weave legends that will give vent to these states and not suppress them. By catharsis one might be able to release the pressure operating on the unconscious and free the being within, at least loosen some resonances.

By leaving space for the spectator, by eliminating the junk of sets and crowded detail of over explained narrative, in other words by freeing the stage and giving it space the spectator can become part of it and is linked to the events by the demands of his imagination that is interpreting for itself what is happening. He is necessary for our success. We make demands on him to 'read' our symbols. He hasn't got time to think or time to drift. By giving him everything as in conventional theatre he will enjoy the spectator role for a while but eventually he will become oppressed, he no longer 'participates': his imaginative resources become congealed and his mystery depleted, and he will become a stunted conscious being with no power to tap his unconscious resources. The outward manifestations of such theatre are boredom and restlessness, one gets hot and the mind starts to think about a multitude of problems that feast on a neglected brain.

Finally. On the House of Usher.

Edgar Allan Poe

E.A. Poe wrote this story when he was 30, in the Spring of 1839, in Philadelphia.

He was born in Boston, the son of Elizabeth Arnold Poe and David Poe, impoverished actors. Poe travelled from Richmond to New York where he intended to marry Sarah Shelton—he was instead found unconscious in a street in Baltimore. He was taken to hospital in a state of delirium and obsessed with imaginary objects on the walls. He died in October 1849 with no conclusive evidence for the cause of his death, whether by drugs or alcohol.

He was truly a great writer who used his own pain and tortured sensibility to write the fantasies imprisoned in his own soul.

D.H. Lawrence on Poe

Moralists have always wondered helplessly why Poe's morbid tales had to be written. They need to be written because old things need to die and disintegrate, because the old white psyche has to be broken down before anything else can come to pass.

There are ghastly stories of the human soul in its disruptive throes.

Moreover they are love stories.

Men live by food but die if they eat too much. Men live by love but die or cause death if they love too much. Love can be terribly obscene . . . . It is love that causes the eroticism of the day. It is love which is the prime cause of tuberculosis. (From *Studies in Classic American Literature,* Heinemann Educational: 1964)

Antonin Artaud on Poe and Usher

Such an affinity as Artaud felt existed between himself and Roderick Usher made him feel that he was not alone in the world; and through association it enhanced his appeal as an actor. Since he could compare his suffering with that of the fascinating Mr. Usher. "My life is that of Mr. Usher and his sinister hovel. The soul of my nerves is disease within and I suffer from this. There is one quality of nervous suffering which the greatest actor in the world cannot bring to life if he has not experienced it. And I have experienced it, I think, as Roderick Usher had."

The Fall of the House of Usher was first performed at the Traverse Theatre by the London Theatre Group for the 1974 Edinburgh Festival, and subsequently at the Hampstead Theatre Club, February 1975.

PLAY ADAPTATION	Steven Berkoff
RODERICK USHER	Steven Berkoff
MADELINE USHER	Shelley Lee
EDGAR/FRIEND	Alfredo Michelson
MUSIC COMPOSED & PLAYED BY	David Ellis
LIGHTING DESIGN	Steven Berkoff & Neil Sanford
DIRECTION	Steven Berkoff

Scene 1

The stage is black. MADELINE lies in a coffin square of light. The doctor walks in slow motion and with a stethoscope. USHER sits stage left in a debilitated posture waiting: 'Perhaps the doctor can resuscitate her.' A beam of light trajects directly his route, the route of the doctor, picking up Usher's lace cuffs on the way. The doctor examines her delicately—is there any hope. As he puts the stethoscope on her body a scream suddenly tears out of her mouth. The effect is shocking after the slow walk which normally takes five minutes to cross twenty feet, and if successful should terminate the life of one member of the audience. This image is a coda of the play.

Scene 2

A blue light now shapes the emaciated figure of USHER dressed in white silken robes and black velvet—a face like enamel; white make-up and green painted eyes. He pours a glass of wine so slowly that one can hear every drop fall into the glass from the back of the Coliseum. The concentration of all his forces is in this act. The light travels through the glass creating a roseate opalescent glow. Usher drains the glass and weakly sets the fine thin glass next to a fluted crystal decanter. (All props should be priceless and precious on stage. Irreplaceable and thus add a degree of tension by their vibrant delicacy and brittleness. The cheap will only coarsen, all costumes must be hand made and costly.)

Scene 3

The servant, masked for anonymity helps USHER to his

Scene 1

MADELINE *lying in square of light as audience enters. She slowly assumes a rigor mortis position. Doctor enters stage right. He approaches her in slow motion bends to listen to her heart. She screams. Blackout.*

Scene 2

USHER *sitting at table stage left. He pours a glass of wine.*

USHER.   I have no fear of danger. Only in its ultimate effect. In terror.

USHER *rises with help of servant and makes his way to centre stage.*

Scene 3

SERVANT.   How are you today sir?

feet. They are walking, but closer to floating as if
weightless. The servant asks how USHER is and USHER
is mortified by the incredible insensitivity of the servant
who could cook his egg for one whole minute longer than
he desires. The servant transforms USHER into the house
and the actor playing USHER becomes vocally and
physically a mimetic reflection of a house. This is only
achieved by an actor who can represent the non-real.
He enacts the pain and age of this house which might
have stood there in a state of decay for centuries. The
House of Usher's speech is the credo of the play—
'All things are sentient' even the stones of this house and
he is the house; he senses the same decay in him as in the
house; in other words he is a total mirror image of the
house—the split in the facade no less parallels his own
splitting psyche.

Scene 4

Description of atmosphere through FRIEND riding on
his way, obeying an urgent summons. (This summons is
done later via a letter rather than have the tedious
sequential narrative of theatre—first comes description—
second comes action.) It just introduces the coming and
keeps an awareness of a being getting nearer and nearer.
Much like film technique we cut from the exterior of the

USHER.   Not very well . . . . My poached egg was a
    minute overdone again Oswald. You know how
    that upsets me.

SERVANT.   Sorry sire. The weather today is still far
    too inclement for your fragile frame.

USHER.   Then I must wrap up. Mustn't I?

SERVANT.   Indeed you must, sir.

        SERVANT *leaves.* USHER *transforms into house.*

USHER.   The House of Usher, my walls are
    Bleak walls, vacant eyelike windows
    Set amidst a few rank sedges,
    White trunks of decayed trees.
    I have stood here for years.
    Minute strands of fungi
    Overhang my whole exterior
    In a fine tangled web-work
    Hanging from the eaves.
    My principal feature is excessive antiquity.
    Discoloration of ages has affected me greatly.
    I am decayed, but not unstable.
    My stones have crumbled yet are held together
    By some invisible power.
    Only the most scrutinizing observer would notice
    A barely perceptible fissure extending from my
    Roof and making its way down
    In a zig zag direction, until it loses itself in
    The sullen waters of the tarn. I hear
    Someone coming to me. To me.
    Make yourself ready house.
    Strengthen yourself to receive him.

        Light on USHER *fades. Light comes up on*
        FRIEND *miming riding a horse.*

Scene 4

FRIEND.   A dull and soundless day.
    In the autumn of the year.
    The clouds hang oppressively low in the heavens.
    I have been passing alone
    On horseback through
    Singularly dreary tracts of country.
    Now as the shades of evening draw on

rider to the interior of MADELINE and USHER, and
lighting will help and does help to demarcate these
differences and separate the time and space.

Scene 5

Introduces MADELINE in her 'light' of disease. A red/
purpureal whirling—the rider meanwhile dissolves to the
'outside'. USHER enters singing her name thinly and high.
They dance to a charming waltz played on the harp. They
come together gently, floating like two butterflies in
flight. They appear almost weightless, fragile—so delicate,
they might chip. They adopt stances in the waltz in which
we read their thoughts. The actor playing USHER should be
a cadaver in appearance yet ruthlessly strong, the strength
of the possessed, weak in effort which then turns to power
when thwarted. The same super-human energy that enables
his twin sister to break the iron hinges of her coffin in
her eventual escape, this kind of strength; people whose
passion and physical energy is not revealed in their
muscular power, but when unleashed demonstrates a
psychic and superhuman force. Therefore the actor must
have the delicacy of a Marceau and the power of an
Olivier—the sensibility and madness of Artaud; in other
words, a thoroughbred, a rarity. He must mime through
suggestability, vocally excite through several octaves and
be demoniacal. (Berkoff, who essayed this role, was not
a typical aesthete Roderick Usher, not specially cadaverous
or brittle, having more the physique of someone who
might have made a reasonable middle-weight or ranking
welter-weight.) USHER permits MADELINE to draw off
his blood, a simple allegorical piece of stage business—
they are feeding off each other and have a vampire
like devotion and need. Also like a vampire in a more
literal sense if you like, she appears dead later and yet is
able to leave the tomb. Also the letter which follows
suggests that he is on his death bed due to an overfed bat
and needs to be rescued.

I find myself within view of the melancholy
House of Usher.

MADELINE *moves into light as* FRIEND *moves
out. She whirls in sickness.* USHER *begins singing
her name as he approaches. When he is at her side
both stop. They begin a surreal dance holding
various positions. While they dance the dialogue is
spoken.*

Scene 5

USHER.   How are you today my dear?

MADELINE.   Not very well Roderick.

USHER.   I'm sorry to hear that. Can I give you something to alleviate it?

MADELINE.   Oh would you Roderick?

USHER.   Of course, my dear.

They stop the dance. USHER *removes the thin
silk scarf around his neck and* MADELINE *descends
on it. When she has had her fill* USHER *pulls away
with a look of horror.* USHER *makes circle to left.*
MADELINE *to right. She comes behind him and
her left hand becomes his pen her right his paper.
Light up on* FRIEND *upstage. The exchange in the
letter is divided between* USHER *and* FRIEND.

Scene 6

Letter

MADELINE always intertwined like ivy or fungi with
USHER becomes the pen writing; a peacock feather will
do for the quill. The friend is seen receiving it as USHER
writes it, thus compressing time and distance. The same
letter is subtly different in each hand.

Scene 7

They unpeel from letter into separate hard sharp pools
of light—separated by areas of darkness—on separate
moons, they are telepathic and move in an integrated
rhythm. They finish each other's sentences and anticipate
the answers to questions. They are both waiting for the
guest to arrive. The rhythm is in slow motion akin to Tai
Chi in its pace but not remotely in emulation of it: since
it is the coarsest thing to single out an element of an
assiduously acquired skill merely to dress something out.
MADELINE mimes the combing of her hair which is

Scene 6

Letter

USHER. Dear friend

FRIEND. So many years have passed.

USHER. Since our last meeting.

FRIEND. My boon companion since childhood.

USHER. From a distant part of the country.

FRIEND. I speak of things a letter . . . wildly demanding.

USHER. Requesting a personal reply. Evidence of nervous agitation.

FRIEND. Bodily illness.

USHER. Mental disorder.

FRIEND. Your company is requested to alleviate

USHER. A malady.

FRIEND. Madness!

USHER. No, not madness. More an ability to see beyond madness . . . are you coming? My good friend? Only friend?

FRIEND. What else can I do?

FRIEND. Only friend.

Light fades on FRIEND. MADELINE *and* USHER *in two spots (stage right and stage left) moving in slow motion.*

Scene 7

USHER. It's dull today.

MADELINE. Dark.

USHER. So silent and still.

MADELINE. The clouds hang oppressively low.

USHER. It is the autumn of the year.

MADELINE. Is your friend coming?

USHER. He said he would—Today's the day he is expected.

naturally more interesting than attempting the combing of real hair since the mime belongs to the audience as well as to space and also she is inviolable and unworried and her hair can cascade down as far as her imagination likes. Mime renders the actor inviolable since they are protected by a metaphor and can stretch and expand to this metaphor. Since mime acts as a metaphor one does not have to worry about dropping any real comb etc. In other words, one does not have to suffer the limitations of the real and can expand in the imaginative and metaphoric world.

MADELINE. He may come tomorrow, it's so dark.

USHER. And difficult to find?

MADELINE. Yes.

USHER. He'll find it. Instructions were very clear. *(Fast soto voce).* It will be good for you, the three of us. It will help to alleviate

MADELINE. The boredom.

USHER. Melancholy, I was about to say. Are you bored Madeline?

MADELINE. No Roderick.

USHER. You said you were. That was the word you used.

MADELINE. No, Roderick. It was only a slip of the tongue.

USHER. I'll ring for Oswald.

> SERVANT *mimes walking through the house as* MADELINE *and* USHER *continue a broken conversation.*

USHER. Such fun we'll have. In the evenings we can play games.

MADELINE. And tell stories. Does he dance, Roderick?

USHER. I seem to remember he did. But the doctor said . . .

MADELINE. He said that four times already.

USHER. You must obey his instructions

MADELINE. But the tablets did nothing

USHER. You didn't take them . . . regularly

MADELINE. They had such a bitter taste

USHER. Sometimes bitter things are good for you.

MADELINE. If you only knew how wearying it is for me, day after day.

USHER. I can Madeline, you tell me day after day.

> SERVANT *opens last set of doors, then enters their room.*

Scene 8

(a)   I'll ring for Oswald

The servant once again masked receives the call on
the bell upstage (the harp) and while the scene
downstage continues, the servant takes five minutes
to walk through the house, thus he delineates the
size of the house by walking through acres of
corridors, up miles of stairs and opening countless
doors. This actor naturally must have a sternly
clean mimetic technique and comic skill closer to
the harlequin than the burlesque: even USHER
through his torment creates a mildly comic and
ironic figure at times, as if his extra-ordinary
sensitivity was a parody on the delicate and the
aesthetic. The servant also plays the FRIEND and
should have a clear ringing voice as he must also
carry the narrative and be highly sensitive to
USHER's moods and not appear ill at ease when
MADELINE and USHER are having their fits, but be
sympathetic, flow with them, understand and help:
after all if their FRIEND was a dolt, USHER would
not have invited him. The servant continues his
walk through the house whilst MADELINE and
USHER are continuing with their scene, thus
compressing two spaces.

(b)   The servant enters and opens the window. The
stage is lit by the eery fuliginous light of the outside
world. Their voices make the cries of the wind. He
shuts the window and exits on USHER's command.
This is to prepare himself to enter shortly as the
FRIEND, but perhaps the whole thing is a masquerade
and the servant is 'playing' the friend for USHER.
Perhaps USHER *has* no friend . . . (this is only an
errant conjecture and not an intention).

Scene 8

(a)

SERVANT.   You rang?

USHER.   *(Gives soundless instructions to* SERVANT
finishing with) . . . and see if he is coming.

SERVANT.   Certainly sir.

SERVANT *walks forward and mimes opening the*
casement windows. MADELINE *and* USHER
stand behind him moving as if blown in a wind.

(b)

SERVANT.   Your guest is late.

USHER.   No sign?

SERVANT.   I see only trees and mist.

USHER.   No sound of hooves? I thought I heard . . .

SERVANT.   No. No. You heard only the wind. The
clouds are heavy with rain.

USHER.   Thank you Oswald. I don't want a weather
forecast.

SERVANT.   Anything else sir?

USHER.   Yes. Leave us . . . please.

MADELINE and USHER.   *(Together. Rythmic)* I'm
sure he'll come Madeline—perhaps he couldn't
find it—and is struggling now in fact. I can almost

Scene 9

The FRIEND is seen riding his horse. (In filmic terms
we have cut back to shot of rider after interposing scene,
or cut to exterior.) MADELINE and USHER have
dissolved back to accompany him as a vocal subliminal
sub-text—the house speaking if you like, and speaking
the thoughts of the friend the subconscious fears as he
approaches the house. They recede to darkness just two
sepulchral figures, their voices lightly ringing out. The
friend enters, a huge gothic archway. The doors creak
open like an indescribably ancient rotting edifice.
MADELINE and USHER pooled in dim spots. They are
effectively looking out from within whilst he is looking
up from without.

hear him. I feel sure . . . can almost hear him . . ..
YES.

SERVANT *leaves. Lights up on* FRIEND *who
mimes riding a horse. As he speaks* USHER *and*
MADELINE *walk slowly up stage and back to
their original places where they become the house.*

Scene 9

FRIEND.   I feel an utter depression of soul
Which I can compare to no earthly
Sensation more properly than to the after dream
Of a reveller upon opium.
The hideous dropping of the veil.
What is it that so unnerves me
In the contemplation of this House of Usher?
I felt it on first sight. But then, thinking
That a mere different arrangement of the picture
would be
Sufficient to modify, or perhaps anihilate its
capacity for
Sorrowful impression, I rein my horse to the brink
of
A black and sullen tarn. Pestilent vapours. Leaden
hues.
The extensive decay reminds me of old woodwork,
Which has rotted for years in some neglected vault,
Yet no portion of the masonry has fallen. No
crumblings
Of individual stone.

MADELINE and USHER.   CODA.
Yes we are here
We have not crumbled. We are   Sickness
Perfect in our adaptation   Torture
of parts   Soul
In our construction, so   Melancholy
perfect.   Depression
                                  Decay
                                  Grotesque

FRIEND.   Yet there hangs on you an atmosphere
emanating from yourself, an atmosphere that has no
affinity with the air of heaven, but reeks up from
decay. I see a figure moving like the shadow of
a ghost.

Scene 10

Step by step I will conduct you

MADELINE and USHER fluidly move through a config-
uration of rooms suggested by their bodies whilst again
intoning the subtext which relates to the FRIEND whom
USHER now calls EDGAR. The FRIEND as narrator
chillingly describes the interior of the house while
MADELINE and USHER create it and are 'it'. MADELINE
always moves loosely and lightly—a split being, between
house and 'her'—the actress like the actors should mime
well and suggest advanced decay, neurosis and catalepsy,
nerves stretched to their taughtest before the point of
snapping, while at the same time have the vocal and
physical strength to convey it. A high degree of dance
skill is very valuable, if not essential—USHER becomes
the doors, vibrates like the house, becomes corridors,
stairs, melting out of the air until the FRIEND is led in.

MADELINE *and* USHER *change from being the house to two figures drawing the curtain to peer out of the window.*

USHER.   He has arrived. You see Madeline, I said he would come.

MADELINE.   But his face, Roderick, looks a little troubled.

USHER.   We'll soon remedy that.

FRIEND.   I approach a Gothic archway. A servant takes my horse without a word.

During this MADELINE *and* USHER *become a gothic archway and then lower their arms to become a heavy door through which the* FRIEND *enters the house.*
Voices create the sound of ancient door seldom opened.

Scene 10

FRIEND.   Which way?

USHER and MADELINE.   Step by step we will conduct you.

USHER *and* MADELINE *become house.* FRIEND *wanders through them.*

FRIEND.	MADELINE and USHER. *(Sung or whispered)*
Conducted in silence	
Through dark and intricate	
Passages. Everything I encounter	Insufferable
In this house	Melancholy
	Half-pleasurable
Heightens vague sentiments of	Poetic
Forboding	Landscape
The carvings of the ceilings	Depression
Sombre tapestries of the walls	Soul
Ebony blackness of the floor	Afterdream
Phantasmagorical armorial trophies	Opium
Which rattle as I stride	Iciness
Into a room large	Sinking

Scene 11

This sculpturing suggests the setting up of our situation.
Aided by the heavy romantic music of Beethoven's 5th,
(3rd movement) the moulding as if by a high speed
sculptor into the clichéd attitudes of posed painting—
they are shaped ready for dinner—they are manipulated
by USHER as if he has arranged and determined the
whole situation of what is also to ensue.

Scene 12

The family is exceedingly ancient

Valuable piece of plot—pure narrative in original story
and aided by instant picture reinforcement of each line—
the gesture the actor must find should somehow
encapsulate the essence. It is like a cypher image.

With windows long narrow and
     pointed   Sickness
Inaccessible feeble gleams of light   Torture
Make their way through the trellised
     panes. The eye struggles in vain,
Dark draperies hang on the walls.
I breathe an atmosphere of sorrow.
An air of deep irredeemable gloom.
Which way? *(door)*
Which way? *(steps)*
Which way? *(door)*

Scene 11

As the FRIEND *is led through the last door Beethoven's
Fifth Symphony begins. The* FRIEND *and* MADELINE
*are sculpted into seated positions on non-existent chairs.
They begin talking and gesticulating without sound.*
USHER *seats himself and signals to stop the music.*

Scene 12

USHER.   The family is exceedingly ancient.*
       Noted time out of mind for its
       Peculiar sensibility of temperament.*
       Producing through the ages many great works of
          art.*
       Including a passionate devotion
       To the intricacies of musical science.*
       And yet never putting forth any enduring branch.*
       The entire family lies in the direct
       Line of descent.*
       Refining its artistic powers until
       They fester like that water
       Which will soon seep under the door.

     (* At each of these places MADELINE *and* FRIEND
     *make a cypher image of the phrase which has been
     said.)*

Scene 13

After these hard images—the stage melts from
their isolated spots into a thick creamy amber. They
slowly walk to the friend from these spots—light pours
down. They repeat the greeting three times, suggesting
how Usher would really like to meet him. The first is
lethargic, which could be real, the second is how he
would like to be, vigorous alive and strong, and perhaps
in the past once was; the third is what generally might
be a normal way of greeting a friend.

Scene 14

During Dinner

The harp strikes a percussion lightly for the dinner scene
which develops tension, they move only inches, eyes
move only fractions of an inch. They are separate again
in their white hard spots which mumify them as if in
plastic. MADLINE drifts into her own world. A harsh
whispered sub-text is ensuing between MADELINE and
USHER 'To behave properly, smile, don't eat with your
fingers' and various admonitory injunctions to her
which the FRIEND partially and politely ignores. The
tension winds up until the confusion becomes comic
and all anwers to questions regarding the weather are
grotesquely comic due to the hysteria of a person
adjusting to table talk after years of isolation and the
solipsistic relationship such as exists between MADELINE
and USHER. The text should act like music with the
precise timings between phrases and comments.
Confusion—which tends to be improvised—surrounds
the words Rumania, which USHER gets stuck on, and
Bohemia, the real country of origin of the FRIEND.

Scene 13

USHER. I greet you with my usual vivacious warmth.

FRIEND. Which has much in it of the constrained effort of ennui.

USHER. But perfectly sincere.

> *This greeting is repeated three times. Each time all three leave their non existent chairs and shake hands then return to the chairs with complete neutrality. The first greeting is formal and slow, the second very open and cheerful. The third, bubbly, slightly nervous, and childlike.*

> *After the third greeting all three return to their chairs. The dinner conversation has extended silences.* USHER *and* FRIEND *mime eating and drinking.* MADELINE *picks at her food and her mind drifts away.*

Scene 14

Sub text

FRIEND. Three days it took me to get here.

USHER. Do you hear that Madeline? Three days, just to come and see us, how very nice of him, how very nice.

FRIEND. Six changes of Horse.

USHER. My word, six changes of horse, you must be exhausted—I am sure the horses must be exhausted too.

FRIEND. Dreadful weather.

USHER. Yes, for this time of the year.

FRIEND. Oh, why?

USHER. Due to the nature of the terrain, the marshes attract a rather pestilential climate.

FRIEND. How interesting.
    Where I come from *(*USHER *begins coughing)*

I said where I come from *(Coughing)* Where I come from.

USHER. Rumania.

FRIEND. No, Bohemia.

USHER. Of course we wrote|to you in Bohemia—
didn't we Madeline. They're very similar.

FRIEND. *(Alarmed)* Pardon?

USHER. *(In confusion)* I mean the words not the
countries, just the words. Probably the countries
could not be more *dis*-similar—I meant—just the
words.

FRIEND. *(Continues)* Yes, I was saying where I come
from in Bohemia the weather . . .

(USHER *has interrupted him with a coughing fit.*
MADELINE *stares horrified.* USHER *continues to*
MADELINE *in a harsh whisper.)*

USHER. Stop staring at me—Sorry *(to* FRIEND)
I do beg your pardon, you were saying that in
Rumania

FRIEND. Bohemia!

USHER. Of course BOHEMIA—They're very similar.
I mean the words not the countries. Possibly the
countries could not be more dissimilar. Oh please,
please continue—you were saying that in . . .
*(He hesitates still confused whether it is Rumania
or Bohemia)*

FRIEND. *(Firmly)* Bohemia—the weather at this time
of year is . . .

(USHER *again goes into a coughing fit that looks
like the beginning of a cataleptical fit and which
prevents the termination of* EDGAR's *sentence.
This develops in* EDGAR *a great determination to
finish it.
Continues again to* MADELINE, *soto voce)*

USHER. Don't stare at me like that! *(To* FRIEND)
Please continue. A momentary fit. It will soon
pass.

FRIEND. *(Very fast)* The weather in my country at
this time of the year is very sunny and warm—very
warm! Very warm and sunny.

Scene 15

Besides I Am Attached to this House

This is USHER's credo on the sentience of the house,
which is his prison and his snail's shell. USHER's thoughts
are spoken out loud, as are those of the FRIEND. They
are in isolation. The light reflects the febrile haunting of
USHER's mind, pondering his attachment to everything
old and decayed around him as if inseparable from
himself, as though joined to its foundations by nerve
fibres. He expresses his belief in the sentience of inorganic
things: thus the stones of this house live in a manner of
speaking, perhaps the dead waves of past occupants have
imbedded themselves in the walls and have become the
family legacy. MADELINE wanders around in sympathy
with USHER. the FRIEND is still, quite still, strong,
gazing at him, astonished by the change the years have
made, and imploring him that the leaving of the house will
improve his health, unaware of the inherited disease of
imbred generations, and the fevered clinging to dead
securities which can only be severed by death.

USHER. Did you hear that Madeline?
The weather at this time of the year in *(Again hesitates—his mind can't grasp the difference between Bohemia and Rumania—pauses for a few seconds—then says uncertainly)*—Bohemia is sunny and warm—How very nice—I don't know when we last had a ray of sunshine here—do you Madeline? (MADELINE *struggles to remember)*
You see its been so long—she can't remember either. (MADELINE *seems on the brink of coming to consciousness but drifts away again)*

FRIEND. Well in that case you both must come to pay me a visit.

USHER. I'd like to but I can't. Not in my condition. How could I?

Scene 15

USHER. Besides I am attached to this house. The grey stones live, in a manner of speaking. Not just the fungi that over-spread them. Not just the dark waters of the tarn. Not just the decayed trees, but the walls themselves.
The result is discoverable in that silent yet terrible influence of the House which has made me what I am.

FRIEND. I look on him with horror. He has altered beyond belief. Are you the same person that I once knew. Cadaverous expression. Ghastly palor of the skin, eyes luminous beyond comparison yet sunken in two dark sockets. Your hair, once so long and fine now clings with lifeless form about your head. You smile. You smile and I cannot recognise the monster which hides behind your teeth. You have altered beyond belief.

We all change a little.

During USHER's *next speech* MADELINE *is behind him echoing his words with gestures of hands and arms.*

Scene 16

We all Change a Little

A humorous downbeat—the sickly weaving of light
has cross faded to 'normal' unguent amber—'We all
change a little'—as if their thoughts had been private and
all EDGAR had said was 'You look different old boy'.
USHER explains his state in a long speech about his
senses that have grown so attenuated and acute through
family legacy and inbreeding. This condition renders all
life intolerable, so unbearable are all impressions except
the mildest. USHER speaks slowly and deliberately,
reaching into his guts for sounds that onomatopoeically
serve as a meaning—stretching the words almost into
visceral images—flowing through these images as if his
breath had produced an ether which also hypnotically
ensnares EDGAR like some heavy perfume. MADELINE
floats and moulds to USHER balletically yet abstractedly
suggesting identification with his thoughts by her arms
and hands that lift and fall about USHER. Here the
sensitivity of the two players reveal themselves in moments
bordering on the arabesque and the grotesque. The two
move almost telepathically, so utterly sensitive are these
twins—one to another—sharing each others pleasures and
pains—that the actors playing them should preferably be
lovers, or about to be at some time during the rehearsal
or have at least tasted the pleasure of each other's bodies.
The light is blue-green from overhead plus purple from
the sides—the harp played exquisitely by a virtuoso player
reiterates and emphasizes.

Scene 17

Besides I have a Sister

The floating body of MADELINE freezes behind USHER—
USHER reveals himself as if she had only just been
introduced. She becomes a still image like a manifested
thought of his, a shimmering image of decay under a hot
red light. As he says 'frequent though transient affection
of a partially cataleptical nature'. MADELINE enacts her fits

Scene 16

USHER.   You see here the result of a family evil,
         brought about through much inbreeding.
         I despair to find a remedy for it.
         My senses are so acute the most insipid food
         alone is endurable to me.
         My troubled flesh can bear garments only of the
         lightest softest texture. The odour of flowers
         oppresses me and my eyes, my eyes are tortured by
         even a faint light.
         Only the delicate tremulous notes of stringed
         instruments are acceptable to my ears.

         I shall perish,
         I must perish
         Thus, thus and not otherwise
         Shall I be lost.
         In this unnerved
         In this pitiable condition
         I feel that the moment will
         Sooner or later arrive when
         I must abandon life and reason together
         In some struggle with the grim phantasm,
         FEAR

FRIEND.   You must leave this house

USHER.   How can I? These walls are my skin. This room
         is my heart. Besides, I have a sister.

Scene 17

Light change. USHER *steps aside leaving* MADELINE
in a frozen position.

USHER.   My last and only relative. A tenderly beloved
         sister..
         The horror of her illness far outweighs mine.
         She approaches the end of her days.
         Her passing will leave me so hopeless

in this harsh red light—like USHER in his previous speech
about his senses, EDGAR is caught. He is caught in her
own light as if in her own atmosphere. He burns himself
in it; like a moth to a candle flame he is drawn to her.
Light flickers in sympathy to her state, USHER is alarmed
at this fit and intones 'to bed Madeline—to bed'.
He reaches up and tears down a dripping silken fabric
which could have previously suggested the fabrics of the
house and now becomes both an image of her winding
sheet and soft cocoon as if the bed had come to her and
she spins around this until she is mumified.

Scene 18

Do you regard me with Dread

USHER answers questions although they are directed at
EDGAR. In her confusion MADELINE believes she is
dancing with USHER. USHER sings the words with
astonishment to suggest the enormity of his passion by
the crude symbol of the anguished vocal power of his
voice.

and frail.
The last of the ancient race of the Ushers.

FRIEND.   But what is her illness?

USHER.   A gradual wasting away of the person.
Frequent though transient affections of a partially
cataleptical nature.
She has born it all refusing to take to her bed.
We do not talk openly.

During this time MADELINE *is going through
spasmodic fits and tremblings. Whenever* USHER
or the FRIEND *come near her they begin to
tremble as well.*

FRIEND.   Openly?

USHER.   Face to face
Lips moving, sounds issuing forth.
She succumbs to the power of the destroyer.
Take your last look.
You'll see her no more

USHER *calms her by wrapping her in a white
translucent cloth. When she is cocooned she begins
to dance with the* FRIEND.

Scene 18

MADELINE.   Do you regard me with dread?

USHER.   With astonishment.

MADELINE.   He regards me with astonishment.
What do you see?

USHER.   A tenderly beloved sister.

MADELINE.   Do you love me Roderick?

USHER.   With astonishment.

MADELINE.   What do you see?

USHER.   Catalepsy, dread wasting, disease.

MADELINE.   Take your last look. You'll see no more.

(The FRIEND *begins to pull the cloth away and
she spins out of it to* USHER. USHER *and*

Scene 19

This is the end of Section 1 or the first movement.

Section A

The house and interior have been described as well as
the inhabitants. Now begins the function of companion-
ship for which the FRIEND has been called. The Bach
Partita weaves in and out of their activities which pass
slowly. They seem to float around the stage, almost
weightless. 'The days pass one by one'—it is a dance,
slowly performed as a series of mimed events which
becomes a tapestry of delicate activity, you could
almost say the activities and proclivities of the people
as opposed to description. USHER paints MADELINE
into a series of poses—his gestures magic her into shape
like an animated cartoon, then he paints the FRIEND—
the painting should develop by stages until USHER can
paint MADELINE no more. She refuses or cannot be
painted into the elegiacal image that he wishes and he
destroys it. EDGAR then attempts to paint them both.
They form into an image which he finds repellent. The
image then breaks up.

Section B

Usher now takes MADELINE and plays her like an
instrument; a cello—she sings some lines from Poe's poem
'The Haunted Palace' in a whine-like dirge. He holds his
sister, cradling her in his arms and uses her arm like a bow,

MADELINE *wander around the stage until he*
places her in a spot stage left. While they talk they
paint her and she assumes the positions their
brushes direct. During the whole of The Days Pass
section a Bach partita is played)

FRIEND. The days pass one by one
 We do not mention her name
 We will not mention her name   (USHER *painting*
 We paint together   MADELINE *and*
 We paint each other   FRIEND)
 We paint.

Scene 19

Section A

FRIEND. And when I turn to my own
 attempts I have a
 single idea
 which will not change
 as I wish
 will not assume the mood   (FRIEND *paints*
 that would improve its   MADELINE)
 lot.
 I begin to fear to touch
 even with my lightest brush
 In case the flesh falls loose
 like fine dust.

Section B

Wandering begins again. USHER *and* MADELINE
stop in spot stage right. She becomes a stringed instru-
ment which he plays.

in fact, this is how they use each other, they play
each other.

Section C

'The days pass one by one'—they now seem to float
together all three like planets in separate orbits, weaving
around each other in their particular trajectories. USHER
poses a laugh, as if suggesting some forced jollity—they
are playing games—EDGAR hands (mimes) a pack of
cards to USHER which USHER beautifully shuffles
and presents them each with a card. He then hides a card
in the pack and after some more ceremonial shuffling
picks a card from the top which is the wrong one. This is
suggested by EDGAR's shaking of his head. USHER
continues offering EDGAR more cards which are all
wrong—the trick has failed. USHER throws them down
in despair. If the mime here is acutely accurate the
scene should be both comic and painful and the
audience should be able to see each and every card, feel
the size and weight of the pack, and understand exactly
what USHER is doing.

Section D

'The days pass one by one'—now a chess game ensues
with MADELINE watching—again EDGAR defeats
USHER, he is now demented by his failure and destroys
the illusion. MADELINE is always floating around the
circumference of their activities, always there, sometimes like a shadowy figure, sometimes close to them,
always hovering.

Scene 20

May I tell you something Edgar

This text about remote regions of the Earth aptly describes
USHER's condition, and is a key to the maladies
of genius as a bed-fellow to madness by the proximity of
genius to intense and neurotic perception. This could of
course be an absolutely accurate description of Edgar
Allen Poe himself. What is one man's madness is another
man's vision. Again EDGAR is caught in the spell of USHER

Section C

FRIEND.   The days pass one by one.
  Her name is not mentioned
  I try to drown my mind in
  Roderick's strange music.
  His family all were talented musicians.
  Spinning a tuneful web across
  their mental shadows. And yet,
  though I have never heard her voice, I
  seem in his improvised dirges, in his
  wildest airs,
  I seem to hear her sing.

Section D

(MADELINE *attempts to sing)*

FRIEND.   The days pass one by one.

Scene 20

USHER.   May I tell you something Edgar . . . May I?
  (Leaning close to FRIEND*)* In remote regions of
  the earth where sunlight is in constant struggle
  with darkness, one step nearer the light and you
  have genius. One step nearer the dark and you have
  madness. Between the two is an indefinable region.
  Do you know what I mean Edgar—do you?

who melts around him and eventually takes hold of
him physically—EDGAR resists this information and the
danger that it implies but is gripped by the iron-like
talons of USHER who is possessed by this idea and
wishes to imbue it into EDGAR who rather than flow
with the idea is a rationalist and a bourgeois, and as far
as he mentally resists the idea, symbolically and
physically resists it.

Scene 21

They continue passing time in the tastes of USHER's
whims and are offered books to read. Each of these
books is of a specific and phantasmagoric nature—
MADELINE and EDGAR become the book and as the
titles are wrenched out of USHER's throat the two enact
the essence of the book in one single image. The light
reinforcing the image. These images, grotesque as they
are flow from the mind of USHER inspired by what he
reads into them until he is eventually reading the very book
of the play he is now in—*The Fall of the House of Usher.*
EDGAR becomes the book. USHER reads his own past
and eventually the book, after a struggle, closes. Closed
by EDGAR who wants no part of it but USHER
attempts to read on desiring perhaps the answers to the
future but is over-powered by EDGAR who does not
wish to see that far.

Scene 21

USHER. Let's devote our time to reading books. Books.
These books form no small part of the mental
existence of Usher, and were, as might have been
expected in strict keeping with his desire for
phantasm. Search the words for their thoughts.
Crack them open and reveal·the creatures crawling
within.

(FRIEND *and* MADELINE *have mimed removing
a book from the shelf and turning over page after
page. As* USHER *reads the titles they enact
characters of each.*)

USHER. Ververt et Chartreuse by Gresset
The Belphegor of Machiavelli
Heaven and Hell by Swedenborg
The Subterranean Voyage of Nicholas Klimm
The Chiromancy of Robert Flud
Journey into the Blue Distance of Tieck
City of the Sun by Campanella

One favourite volume was a small octavo edition
of the Directorium Inquisitorium by the Arch
Bishop de Gironne. And there were tales of the
African satyrs which Usher would sit perusing for
hours. Above all hammered in vellum with
caligraphic type was 'The Fall of the House of
Usher' by Edgar Allen Poe.

FRIEND *begins reciting from the beginning of the
play with arms open as if he is a book.* USHER
*takes over the words and recites them more and
more quickly as the book begins to close.*

FRIEND. During the whole of a dull, dark, and soundless
day in the autumn of the year when the clouds

Scene 22

The following day Madeline Expires

MADELINE is trapped like a stoat in a glare of a torch
as her sickness (red wine lights) hit her. Suffering her
torments unheeded and unheard, perhaps, since USHER
was outside in the grounds possibly he could not hear
her scream but of course he must hear her, but can no
longer bear it, can no longer tolerate her agonised cries.
As she twists in her cataleptical torment, they, the two
men, in contrast walk slowly in normal white light, the
exterior of the house, while MADELINE is dying in her
death ray red. The contrast is shocking. 'Two physicians
were called'. These two men draw hats out of the air and
act/narrate the doctors who enter the house. Her heart
beats are fearful and pounding, and they were only just
in time to catch the last fleeting drops of her heart which
they literally do, as if some incubus had departed from
her wasted and shivering body—the heart beats, oscillated
electronically, are a dreadful, pounding externalisation of
her inner agony. USHER (as doctor) catches her heart
as if catching a butterfly in a net and crushes it in his
hands. The beating stops—the doctors leave. The pounding
of her heart must shake the building to be really

hang oppressively low in the heavens, I had been making my way on horseback, passing through singularly dreary tracts of country. Now as the shades of evening draw on I find myself within view of the melancholy house of Usher.

USHER.   Bleak walls, vacant eyelike windows, set amidst a few rank sedges a few white trunks of decayed trees I have stood here for years, minute strands of fungi overhang my whole exterior in a tangled web work from the eaves my principle feature is excessive antiquity, discoloration of ages has affected me greatly. I am decayed but not unstable, my stones have crumbled yet are held . . . .

Book closes. Blackout.
Light up on MADELINE *in her death throes.*

Scene 22

USHER.   *(In narrator tone)*   The following day Madeline expired.
The maladies of catalepsy had claimed her at last—her screams rang through the entire House—making even the stone walls tremble.

FRIEND.   Usher and his friend were out walking in the gardens.

USHER.   A rare moment of sunshine taken advantage of.

FRIEND.   And were too far away to hear her cries. The friend certainly could not, and if Usher did, he made no sign.
(As USHER*)* Not a breath of wind today. Just the slightest whisp of cirrus clouds.

USHER *and* FRIEND *are downstage right and left. They put on imaginary top hats and impersonate doctors. Walk to centre stage and open door to* MADELINE's *room. She remains perfectly still as they walk towards her, listen to her heart, catch the last drops and walk out.*

effective and convey to the audience what dying is like.
If the heart beats continue too long, a member of the
audience may find his own heart sympathising in tempo
to the taped beat. This has been scientifically proven, and
then when the tape stops at MADELINE's death this
particular person in the audience may also suffer the
same effects of a sympathetic heart stopping. There is no
solution to this but up to now casualties have been low.

Scene 23 *and* Scene 24

See here. At last he is to Speak of her.

MADELINE has returned to darkness—EDGAR and
USHER, two separate pools of light, left and right
stage. USHER screams/sighs/cries out the name of his
sister. First an outward cry sung which develops into an
inward scream of anguish into a high falsetto. At the
end his voice returns to deep resonance as if restored
by a purge. As if the voice had returned from a voyage
into hell. He invokes the help of his friend to carry her
body downstairs where he wishes to keep her interred
for two weeks before the final burial. No real
explanation except to be 'near' her—or rather to
enjoy her screams as she awakes and attempts to tear
herself out of the coffin. He loves her with such a
sickening love that he really wants to punish her; this is
my conjecture. If she is in the vaults of the house rather
than buried in the family grounds, even outside USHER's
phenomenal hearing, it must be to make sure she is dead.
Under a ton of earth outside surely there she is unredeem-
able, *but* merely in the coffin downstairs, if she did
scream, Usher could recover her and she would revive
if the cataleptic state had deceived them into believing
her dead, and thus be lifted out of the coffin . . . but...

USHER.   Two doctors were called.

FRIEND.   But were too late to do anything.

USHER.   Except make the merest token gesture.

FRIEND.   But were in time

USHER.   To catch the last fleeting drops of her heart.

Scene 23

Doctors leave. Lights out. As lights come up MADELINE *is up stage with her hands across her chest in a death position.* USHER *is wandering about the stage, confused and lost.*

FRIEND.   See here. At last he is to speak of her. I can
      see his lips moving forming the lovely name
      Madeline. But its been so long since he said it that
      he must rehearse it.

Scene 24

USHER *attempts to say her name. Finally he cries out.*

USHER.   Madeline *(Sung)*
      My sister is no more.
      I shall preserve her corpse for two weeks
      Before interment
      The unusual nature of her malady makes me
      featful
      To hurry her to the family burial grounds far
      away from me.
      We must wind our way through the dark entrails
      Of the House, a rank place, stinking bowels of
      The House where the bodies rest against the
      Earth. Will you help me please, will you,
      Please, help please.

Scene 25

Section A

Reuluctantly the FRIEND helps him, not before
issuing a word of warning regarding the nature of
fear. That what you most fear can set the waves of
energy twisting around to cause the event you
most fear.

Section B

They descend into the vaults miming the stairs
accurately demonstrating the illusion of depth—light
changes to opalescent green—one hears the sound
of water dripping and echoing, creaking vaults long
unopened—MADELINE is standing at the back of the
stage in a square of light, suggesting the coffin she
is about to be deposited in. The two men move their
hands over the light which fades and transfers itself to a
square of light on the ground, effectively suggesting at
the same time the lifting of her body into the tomb.
MADELINE vanishes into the actual coffin standing
upright or bird's eye view from the audience. Only the
space remains—that is the oblong square of light. They
mime the closing of the lid over the space and the light
gradually fades as if from her point of view. The lid
closing extinguishes all light from outside and we are put
inside her coffin with her. Then USHER orders his friend
to 'screw down the lid'. This contradicts what might
have been USHER's desire in having his beloved sister
near to him—to be able to help her leave the coffin if he
hears her cry—since USHER must know that catalepsy
can effect the semblance of death. So we must surmise
that he wants to hear her agony. The last exquisite
sensation left to him—or taking our original theory of
vampirism, he wants to rid himself of her for all time.

Scene 26

As USHER climbs out of that dark inferno, he ponders
on the fact that there was a faint flush on her cheek, a
mockery of a smile upon her lips, and has time to be
moved aesthetically by her beauty while mourning her
death.

Scene 25

Section A

FRIEND.   Fear, by anticipating terrible events, has a
   way of bringing about those very events.

   USHER *and* FRIEND *mime climbing down into the
   vaults. Sounds of dripping water and creaks and
   groans.*

Section B

USHER and FRIEND.   Vaults
   Long unopenend
   Oppressive
   Smell
   Damp
   Lightless
   Remote
   Stinking

USHER.   Once a dungeon

FRIEND.   Now

USHER.   A place where the bodies of the family rest
   against the earth.
   What you hear are the waters of the tarn seeking
   to reclaim their former territories.

   *When they have reached the vaults they
   metaphorically take the figure of* MADELINE *and
   place her in the coffin. She is standing, her arms
   crossed, eyes, closed, at the back of the stage.*

USHER.   Screw down the lid

   Sound of lid closing. They begin to climb.

Scene 26

USHER.   We deposit our mournful burden
   Within the region of horror,
   A faint flush, the mockery of
   A smile upon her face
   The maladies of catalepsy
   So terrible in death, and yet
   So beautiful.

Scene 27

Darkness—we are in the vault—horror upon horror.
She awakes—the black gauze which she stands behind
representing the stern black coffin becomes invisible,
revealing through the top and back light the figure of
MADELINE. She doesn't know where she is. Gradually
the stark knowledge of what her mad brother has done
seeps in. She panics. Mimes the solid confines with her
hands, tries to claw at the sides of her tomb. She
accurately suggests the square confines of solid material.
The harp transmits the terrible and awful scratching.
She is locked and fastened in—of course we are sure
that USHER must hear this.

Scene 28

Several Days of Bitter Grief Having Elapsed

The previous scene fades leaving the black tomb like
a monolith always down there in the vaults but always
with us— USHER performs this next scene as if limp,
lifeless as a puppet, fed by the energy of the narrator
who is EDGAR. EDGAR works the strings, USHER is
manipulated. More than merely a novel way of present-
ing narrative, it also suggests the dehumanised USHER,
victim of all pressures, acute fears, doubts and
regrets—a lifeless form. Also he appears to be listening
for something, struggling with some oppressive secret.
The puppet master leaves USHER. USHER then melts
from puppet into human. He weeps for his sister and
thrashes in a welter of high pitched remorse—he moves
from the circular puppet light of the ring master into
a hard cross light from two opposing beams. This tracks
a route for his steady pacing—EDGAR upstage looks up
at the ceiling, thereby suggesting the two planes of
space in one—USHER upstairs, EDGAR downstairs,
listening to his steady pacing. EDGAR's eyes move
across the ceiling following the sounds of USHER's
steps. USHER aware always of being watched
perversely changes his pace, whispering to an unseen
audience his complaints about being listened to.
When USHER stops he seems to be listening to something—fearful—he freezes as if in ice, bends down to

Scene 27

MADELINE *has slipped behind a gauze curtain. Lights up on her waking in coffin. She mimes pounding and scratching at coffin lid, struggling to escape. Blackout.*

Scene 28

USHER *moving about the stage with great lassitude.*

FRIEND.   Several days of bitter grief having elapsed,
      an observable change came over the features of
      the mental disorder of my friend.
      His ordinary manner had vanished, his ordinary
      occupations are neglected or forgotten . . . .
      He roams from chamber to chamber with hurried,
      unequal and objectless step. The palor of his
      countenance has assumed, if possible, a more
      ghastly hue, and the luminousness of his eyes
      has utterly gone out. The occasional huskiness of
      his tone is heard no more, and a tremulous quaver,
      as if of extreme terror characterises his utterance.
      There are times when I think his unceasingly
      agitated mind is labouring with some oppressive
      secret, to divulge which he struggles for the
      necessary courage.

USHER.   She is gone.
      Finished frozen. Dead! Why therefore can I not
      forget? I move through these ancient rooms,
      searching for fragments of her broken spirit that
      I might take them in a mental trap and carry
      them down to where her body lies. Still body.
      Still born. Here but not here.
      But he is always here, listening.

the floor, puts his ear to the ground and screams. We
know he hears what we are about to see and the coffin
lights up presently.

Scene 29

MADELINE demented and pounding on the coffin
accompanied by the most horrific screams rending
through the theatre—screams almost inhuman—her ,
light, sulphurous, murky and deadly—USHER barely
seen—his ear to the floor listening from the depths to
their fearful sound, the sounds of animals having their
entrails torn out—the light fades on her and the scene
transfers to a storm—the friend, EDGAR, is in bed—a
sheet represents the bed.

Scene 30

Storm

Paul Watts, our sound technician, assembled a storm
for us on tape. It grows and swells into a fearful breaking
of the heavens. The effect is like a series of hallucinations
inside USHER's skull. The house shakes and USHER is
hurled across the stage. In the midst of the storm which
should resemble the storm scene in *Lear*, we see MADELINE
and USHER and the FRIEND caught in terror. In a literal
sense this is untrue since in the original story there is no
sound or lightning since the house glows in a ghastly
luminous vapour suggestive of the death pangs of the
house itself reaching up from the deep fetid depths of the
tarn. Yet dramatically the storm works better since it
gives reinforcement to the agony of the house and its

USHER *begins pacing.* FRIEND *looks up as if he is listening to* USHER *pace in room above him.*

FRIEND. What is your secret Usher?

USHER. I have none to tell. I roam

FRIEND. From chamber to chamber with unequal objectless step.

USHER. The mockery of a smile upon her lips. So horrible in death and yet so beautiful.

Scene 29

USHER *stops pacing. He listens. Listens. Listens. Screams.*

Light up on MADELINE *in coffin. Tape of pounding with nine screams. She struggles to escape.*

Scene 30

STORM. USHER *is thrown about the stage. Occasional light up on* MADELINE.

Storm fades. Light up on FRIEND *hiding behind sheet.*

occupant whose death tremors are marked by the last
feverish excitement—the light leaps and plays across the
stage, sometimes going to blackout, leaving MADELINE
lit in her tomb cutting through the transparent gauze
lid of her coffin. She appears, lit by strokes of lightning,
still standing, waiting, struggling to escape. At the same
time, the FRIEND is seen in his bed covered by his sheet
with one glassy eye staring out like a basilisk terror-
struck. So here we compress the three sections of the
house—USHER, MADELINE and FRIEND.

Scene 31

Night the Seventh

EDGAR—bound tight into a wracking tension, a hard
beam of light tracks along to his bed—it is already
one week since MADELINE has been sealed in her
coffin. A week with little air and no food or water, so
perhaps she may still be living—just. USHER has heard
the storm which rages inside the nightmare of his own
skull. He walks steadily towards EDGAR's room, his step
emphasised by the harp—he wants Edgar to share this
experience with his friend. USHER is frightened. He is
breaking up gradually as surely as the fabric of the
house is beginning to crack.

Scene 32

USHER knocks on EDGAR's door and enters—they occupy
one hard shaft of light. He wishes EDGAR to share
this experience and carries the storm in his hands in the
shape of a cloth, black, attached to two sticks—having
seen an external storm Usher will create his own one. He
will be the manifestation of one. He implores EDGAR to
see it and, as if USHER himself is a manifestation
of inward chaos and upheaval, opens the casement
window and unfurls his stick. It unrolls revealing a simple
black cloth—this is night—dark, no moon or stars yet
everything glows. He spins the stick slowly which

Scene 31

FRIEND.   Night the seventh, or is it the eighth day since
we placed our lady into the deepest vault. I struggle
to reason off this nervousness which comes at me
from all sides. I endeavour to believe that it is due
to the gloomy furniture in this room, to the dark
and tattered draperies which hang to and fro tortured
into motion by a storm, invisible, inaudible, and
so all the more horrific. I hear his footsteps on the
adjoining staircase, he approaches my room, raps at
my door.

USHER *standing outside his room knocks.*

Scene 32

USHER.   May I come in?

(USHER *is carrying a black cloth attached to two
sticks. He begins to unroll it and starts the cloth
spinning and wirling about his head.*)

USHER.   Have you not seen it? How beautiful it is.
Tempestuous and sternly beautiful. A whirlwind
is gathering flowers in our vicinity with iron
fingers. The clouds cling to the very turrets of
the house, no glimpse of moon or stars, no lightning
flash yet everything glows in a faintly luminous

gradually becomes a whirlwind and almost suggests the
wings of a bat or heaving curtains beating against a window.
It spins more and more furiously until EDGAR stops him.
EDGAR rolls the storm up and offers to control his friend
by telling him a story about Ethelred and the dragon.

Scene 33

This is a simple tale performed or recited from two
chairs and with two hard overhead profile spots—they
both face out front, sculptured in this light, and EDGAR
proceeds to tell USHER the story. This is in fact not
only a love story in one sense of the romantic tryst and
the killing of the dragon, but a neat doubling of the
events mirroring MADELINE breaking out of the tomb.
It should be told simply—quite still—like a fairy tale, with
only the delicate accompaniment of the glockenspiel.
The events of breaking open the hermit's door and the
death cry of the dragon in the story are doubled by
MADELINE, revealed in her sepulchral light within
the coffin. The FRIEND continues, dimly aware of the
sounds eerily echoing the events of the story—as if by
coincidence. USHER during this time has gone into a
stupor—possessed by that sound that only he is able to
interpret.

gaseous exhalation hanging like velvet over Usher.
Have you not seen it?

*(Whirling cloth settles. USHER holds it in front of
him and FRIEND begins to roll the cloth up.)*

FRIEND.   You must not—you shall not behold this.
These appearances which bewilder you are merely
electrical phenomena, not uncommon, or it may
be that they have their ghastly origin in the dank
miasma of the tarn. Let me close the casement. This
air is chilling and dangerous to your frame. I will
tell you instead a story; you will listen and so we will
pass this terrible night together.

(FRIEND *and* USHER *get two chairs. Story is told
in near stillness,* USHER *only slightly reflecting
the words of the* FRIEND.)

Scene 33

FRIEND.   You remember how our hero Ethelred,
having sought in vain for a peaceable entrance
into the hermit's dwelling, proceeds to make good
an entrance by force.
Ethelred, who was by nature of a doughty heart,
and who was now mighty withall, on account of
the powerfulness of the wine which he had drunken,
waited no longer to hold parley with the hermit,
who was in sooth of an obstinate and maliceful
demeanour, but, feeling the rain upon his shoulders,
and fearing the rising of the tempest, he uplifted
his mace outright, and with blows, made quickly
room in the planking of the door for his gauntleted
hand, and then he so cracked and ripped and
tore all asunder that the noise of the dry and hollow
sounding wood alarmed and reverberated through-
out the forest.

Light on MADELINE *struggling to escape*

And Ethelred now entering within the door was
sore enraged and amazed to perceive no sign of
the maliceful hermit; but, in the stead thereof, a
dragon of a most scaley and prodigious demeanor,
with a tongue of fire and with jaws of steel which
sate in guard before a palace of gold with a floor

Scene 34

Not Hear it— Yes I have Heard it.

The confession comes now at a time which is inevitable—
he must tell it. He has heard her breaking out of the
tomb. He has heard her for days. Is his fear real or did
he enjoy those feeble movements in the hollow coffin—
and could he not have rushed down and released her?
'I dare not' he cried, 'I dared not speak'. Of course he
dared not. The oversensitive fiend murdered her.
Each man kills the thing he loves, and he loved her too
much, so much that his senses could no longer accept
the racking destruction of his psyche. So he, in effect,
made no mistake in the burying—perhaps when he buried
her he hoped she was dead and kept her there just to
make sure—perhaps the sounds were exquisitely painful
and horrible to his unbalanced mind and his intombing
of her could be pure malice. But this is just conjecture.
Now he screams for help—he cries and panics—can even
hear the beating of her heart, heavy and horrible. She
has come for him. A light floods the stage. The shocking

of silver. And upon the wall there hung a shield of
shining brass with the legend enwritten
   Who entered herein a conqueror had been
   Who slayeth the dragon, the shield shall he win.
And Ethelred uplifted his mace, and struck upon the
head of the dragon, which fell before him, and gave
up his pesty breath, with a shriek so horrid and
harsh, and withal so piercing that Ethelred had
fain to close his ears against the dreadful noise of
it, the like whereof was never before heard.
(*Cut to* MADELINE) And now the champion
approached valorously to where the shield was
upon the wall, which in sooth tarried not for his
full coming, but fell down with a mighty, great and
terrible ringing sound.

USHER, *during the story has been listening to
sounds only he hears. Suddenly he becomes trans-
fixed and begins talking insanely. Heartbeats begin.*

Scene 34

USHER. Not hear it?
   Yes I hear it, long—long—long—many minutes, many
   hours, many days have I heard it. Yet I dared not
   speak. We have put her living in the tomb!
   Said I not my senses were acute? I now tell you I
   heard her first feeble movements in the hollow
   coffin . . . I heard them, many many days ago, yet
   I dared not, I dared not speak.
   And now—tonight—Ethelred—the breaking of the
   hermit's door, and the death cry of the dragon, and
   the clangour of the shield.
   Say rather I heard the rending of her coffin, the
   grating of the iron hinges of her prison and her
   struggle within the coppered archway of the vault.
   Oh whither shall I fly? Will she not be here anon.
   Is she not hurrying to upbraid me for my haste?
   Have I not heard her footstep on the stair?
   Do I not distinguish that heavy and horrible beating
   of her heart?
   MADMAN . . !
   MADMAN! I TELL YOU THAT SHE NOW STANDS

apparition of MADELINE appears. She has aged. A
Kubuki death mask is on her face—pale and sickly. She
walks on the borrowed strength of the Devil. Her heart
beats become louder and just before she reaches her
beloved brother, her heart stops dead, but her nerves
have sent the impulses to her brain and she will surely
destroy him as she squeezes the life out of him. She
knew he had murdered her and could hear her cries to
be let out. If not, she may have sadly said 'Roderick
dear, you made a rather clumsy mistake'and forgiven
him. No such ending.

Scene 35

USHER's life is extinguished silently, slowly and painfully. MADELINE returns to her original coffin and
square of light, returns to death. The FRIEND relates
the ending of the house. USHER now as a chorus for himself turns once more into his original image of the house,
trembling like the walls crumbling. And as the FRIEND
says 'The Fissure widens, a noise is heard like the
voice of a thousand waters'—from USHER's throat
comes a horrific sound—more horrible than can be
imagined from a human throat—the sound of decay,
the sound of crumbling walls, sliding into the tarn. The
light fades—the two men leave the stage with its initial
image still intact—the corpse of MADELINE in rigor
mortis.

Black out.

WITHOUT THE DOOR!

Houselights up. MADELINE *makes a very slow floating walk to chair where* USHER *is seated. Her hands move slowly, almost tenderly to his neck. Suddenly she screams and grabs his throat. She returns to original square of light representing a coffin and falls slowly back into it as in the beginning of the play.* USHER *collapses as house.*

Scene 35

FRIEND.   A wild light crosses my path.
  Shoots ahead of me. I turn and see
  A blood red moon, the barely discernable fissure
  Extending in a zig zag direction from roof to
  base.
  The fissure widens. The walls rush assunder.

  A sound is heard like the voice of a thousand
  waters.
  The deep dank tarn at my feet closes sullenly,
  and silently over the fragments,
  of the House of Usher.

 Black out

THE END

Q   What do the following have in common:
Steven Berkoff · Michael Burrell ·
Anton Chekhov · Brian Clark ·
Barry Collins · Eduardo de Filippo ·
Keith Dewhurst · Nell Dunn ·
Charles Dyer · Rainer Werner Fassbinder ·
Donald Freed · Maxim Gorky ·
Richard Harris · Ronald Harwood ·
Roy Kift · Hanif Kureishi ·
Bob Larbey · Tony Marchant ·
Sean Mathias · Mark Medoff ·
Julian Mitchell · Mary O'Malley ·
Caryl Phillips · Manuel Puig ·
James Saunders · Anthony Shaffer ·
Martin Sherman · August Strindberg ·
Peter Terson · Heidi Thomas ·
Brian Thompson · John Wain ·
Hugh Whitemore · Snoo Wilson ·
David Wood · Sheila Yeger ?

A   They're all playwrights, silly!

Q   But what *sort* of playwrights?

———————→